BAS

FAS

FASHION DRAWING

Ethical: aware-
ness/
reflect-
ion/
debate

ava
academia

An AVA Book
Published by AVA Publishing SA
Rue des Fontenailles 16
Case Postale
1000 Lausanne 6
Switzerland
Tel: +41 786 005 109
Email: enquiries@avabooks.ch

Distributed by Thames & Hudson (ex-North America)
181a High Holborn
London WC1V 7QX
United Kingdom
Tel: +44 20 7845 5000
Fax: +44 20 7845 5055
Email: sales@thameshudson.co.uk
www.thamesandhudson.com

Distributed in the USA & Canada by:
Ingram Publisher Services Inc.
1 Ingram Blvd.
La Vergne TN 37086
USA
Tel: +1 866 400 5351
Fax: +1 800 838 1149
Email: customer.service@ingrampublisherservices.com

English Language Support Office
AVA Publishing (UK) Ltd.
Tel: +44 1903 204 455
Email: enquiries@avabooks.ch

ISBN 978-2-940411-15-3

10 9 8 7 6 5 4 3 2 1

Design by Sifer Design

Cover illustration by Cecilia Carlstedt

Production by AVA Book Production Pte. Ltd., Singapore
Tel: +65 6334 8173
Fax: +65 6259 9830
Email: production@avabooks.com.sg

All reasonable attempts have been made to trace, clear and credit the
copyright holders of the images reproduced in this book. However, if any
credits have been inadvertently omitted, the publisher will endeavour to
incorporate amendments in future editions.

1   Illustration by Lovisa Burfitt.

741. 672   HOP
BAT 6814
1 WK

1

Contents

Contents

'*I don't know where I'm going until I actually sit down and draw.*'

Jean Muir

1   Fashion designer and illustrator Lovisa Burfitt describes her drawing style as 'very fast and restless'.

Drawing may be described as an evolutionary process that is fundamental to communicating ideas. This is also true of fashion drawing, with its distinctive nuances and associations with style. The exciting breadth and diversity of what constitutes fashion drawing today is testimony to the creative vision of fashion designers and fashion illustrators alike. It reflects the range and scope of media now available, from a simple graphite pencil to sophisticated CAD programs.

Basics Fashion Design: Fashion Drawing provides a visually orientated introduction to the different drawing styles, techniques and approaches that are taught at colleges and used extensively in the fashion industry. The first part of the book addresses the basic principles of good fashion drawing, including the importance of the ubiquitous fashion sketch in communicating an idea. Understanding fashion proportions in relation to the anatomy of the standing figure is considered in chapter two. The following chapter introduces the distinctive nature and purpose of fashion 'flats' and the linear drawing processes of individual garments. The role of computers to support and enhance the drawing process is also considered and compared to more traditional hand-rendering techniques. The second part of the book covers drawing enhancements, including colour rendering as an important aspect of fashion artwork, collage and mixed media techniques. Finally, fashion drawings for presentation formats and fashion portfolios are explained and visually illustrated.

Perhaps the most defining characteristic of the fashion drawing process, and particularly the fashion sketch, is that it should enable the designer or illustrator to express him or herself. It should give rise to a personal drawing style, much like we have our own handwriting styles. Drawing can take time to establish and a lifetime to perfect. However, it's worth perfecting and it does get better with practice!

How to get the most out of this book

This book is a visually orientated introduction to fashion drawing and illustration. Each chapter provides numerous examples of the different drawing styles, techniques and approaches that are taught on fashion courses and used within the industry.

Throughout the book there are interviews with talented designers and illustrators, each of which offers a different perspective on drawing styles as well as an insight into the fashion industry.

Clear navigation
Each chapter has a clear heading to allow readers to quickly locate areas of interest.

Captions
These provide image details and commentary to guide the reader in the exploration of the visuals displayed.

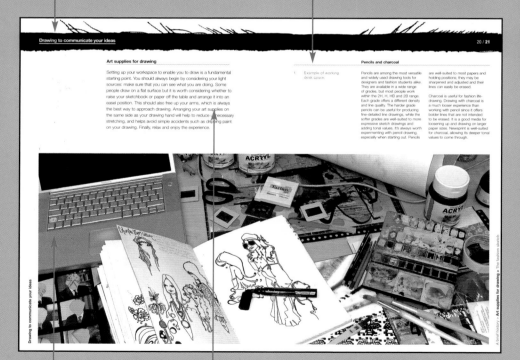

Art supplies for drawing

Setting up your workspace to enable you to draw is a fundamental starting point. You should always begin by considering your light sources: make sure that you can see what you are doing. Some people draw on a flat surface but it is worth considering whether to raise your sketchbook or paper off the table and arrange it into an easel position. This should also free up your arms, which is always the best way to approach drawing. Arranging your art supplies on the same side as your drawing hand will help to reduce unnecessary stretching, and helps avoid simple accidents such as dripping paint on your drawing. Finally, relax and enjoy the experience.

1   Example of working desk space.

Pencils and charcoal

Pencils are among the most versatile and widely used drawing tools for designers and fashion students alike. They are available in a wide range of grades, but most people work within the 2H, H, HB and 2B range. Each grade offers a different density and line quality. The harder grade pencils can be useful for producing fine-detailed line drawings, while the softer grades are well-suited to more expressive sketch drawings and adding tonal values. It's always worth experimenting with pencil drawing, especially when starting out. Pencils are well-suited to most papers and holding positions; they may be sharpened and adjusted and their lines can easily be erased.

Charcoal is useful for fashion life-drawing. Drawing with charcoal is a much looser experience than working with pencil since it offers bolder lines that are not intended to be erased. It is a good media for loosening up and drawing on larger paper sizes. Newsprint is well-suited for charcoal, allowing its deeper tonal values to come through.

Examples
Imagery accompanying the content, visually describing fashion drawing styles and techniques.

Introductions
Special section introductions outline basic concepts that will be discussed.

Fashion Drawing

Headings
These enable the reader to break down text and refer quickly to topics of interest.

Additional information
Box-outs elaborate on techniques discussed in the main text.

Colour forecasting

Selecting colours – or, more specifically, the right colours for a particular season – is crucial in the fashion industry and can mean the difference between success and failure in terms of a label's image and sales. Fashion designers will often visit their suppliers to discuss colours for the coming season and will work closely with their textile partners to develop 'lab dips' and 'strike-offs' for printed textiles. Additionally, the global fashion industry is served by a network of trend and fashion forecasting companies that provide detailed colour analysis, colour direction and market-trend research for fashion and interiors up to two years in advance of the selling season. Companies such as Trendstop, Peclers, Li Edelkoort for Trend Union and Promostyl, among others, are well-respected authorities on colour, each producing a variety of specialist reports for their fashion clients. They also employ fashion-orientated illustrators who contribute to their publications with hand-drawn illustrations alongside CAD artwork and colour presentation flats.

1–8. Colour forecasting and catwalk trend images from Trendstop.

Lab dips
A process whereby a fabric swatch is test dyed to meet an exact colour standard. Lab dips are reviewed in a light box under controlled lighting conditions and may be analysed with a spectrometer.

Strike-offs
A strike-off is a small run of screen-printed fabric, which is used to test the integrity of the screen for accuracy and colour trueness. It also refers to fabric that is printed in new colours or on new grounds with existing screens before a production run.

OLD GOLD 15-0955 TPX

Colouring and rendering

Colour for fashion » Fabric rendering

Chapter titles
These run along the bottom of every page to provide clear navigation and allow the reader to understand the context of the information on the page.

Running footers
Clear navigation allows the reader to know where they are, where they have come from and where they are going in the book.

How to get the most out of this book

1   Line-up illustration by
Gudrun Kloepsch.

'For me drawing is the magic connection between inspiration and expression.'

Jean-Charles de Castelbajec

Drawing starts with imagination before it expresses itself as a practical means of generating or communicating an idea. In fashion this can manifest itself in a variety of ways that are linked to social, artistic and cultural values or influences. This chapter briefly traces the origins of fashion drawing since the late 19th century to its contemporary expression as the modern fashion sketch. The techniques and available art supplies are considered in relation to how fashion drawing has evolved over time as a hand-rendered practice. The sketching process and purpose of sketchbooks are also considered and visually presented to include examples of working drawings and rough sketches, which are taken from a variety of contemporary sources.

This chapter also includes interviews with a commercial fashion designer and an accomplished designer and illustrator to gain additional perspectives on fashion drawing styles, media choices and personal inspirations.

A brief history

Pochoir
A labour-intensive process that was popular in France in the early 20th century, pochoir involved creating a colour print with a series of stencils in which each colour was vividly applied by hand. The numerous stencils had to be carefully placed in order to apply the individual paints (watercolour, gouache, ink) for colour separation.

Gouache
A type of paint that consists of pigment suspended in water. Gouache differs from watercolour in that the particles are larger and the ratio of pigment to water is much higher. It also contains chalk, which makes it heavier and more opaque, with greater reflective qualities.

Tempera
Tempera is a type of paint made by mixing powdered pigments with egg yolk. When dry, it produces a smooth, matt finish.

From the mid-19th century onwards fashion-interest publications such as *La Mode Illustrée*, *Gazette du Bon Ton* and *Modes de Paris* published increasingly sophisticated fashion plates of the styles that emanated from Paris. These drawings became important cultural markers of fashion in their own right and began to influence the aesthetic view of dress styles, as well as to communicate the 'looks' of the day to their readers.

During the late 19th century, Parisian couturiers such as Charles Frederick Worth began to sketch their ideas for private clients. Typically these early examples of fashion drawings aimed for proportional realism, with the garment rendered in great detail.

1

2

1900s–1910s

At the turn of the century, while the prevailing look of the day was controlled by the constricting S-shaped corset, one notable illustrator with a distinctive drawing style defined a look that was referred to as the 'Gibson Girl'. His name was Charles Dana Gibson and his prolific pen-and-ink drawings were widely published and admired. Gibson portrayed an elegant, yet slightly aloof woman who has been variously described as taller, more spirited but altogether feminine.

Following the extreme hourglass silhouette at the turn of the century, fashion details focused on the bust line; the introduction of the sheath corset influenced a new, more elongated silhouette. Fashion drawings were inspired by the art nouveau movement, with an added infusion of theatrical influences and the spectacle of the touring Ballets Russes.

In 1908, couturier Paul Poiret commissioned the young print maker Paul Iribe to draw his gowns for *Les Robes de Paul Poiret*, published in 1909. Using the pochoir process, Iribe applied his vibrant colours to each print using stencils for each colour. It was the first time a couturier had looked to modern art to represent his creations and it redefined fashion illustration.

Watercolour, gouache and tempera were all used during this period as drawings took on a more 'painterly' approach. Watercolour paper or lightweight card was frequently used to prevent the water-based media from buckling the paper. The resulting fashion plates presented vibrant colours and linear clarity.

1920s

During the 1920s the drawing style became more angular and linear in presentation, consistent with the changing silhouette and artistic move towards art deco. The new, 'boyish' figure appeared longer and leaner than before as the prevailing fashions changed.

Drawings began to reflect a frivolity as the new 'flapper' silhouette took centre stage. With the corset abandoned, fashionable women bound their breasts and wore simple slips as the waistline relaxed to hip level. The Japanese kimono became an important stylistic influence and beadwork and fringing often adorned the otherwise simple shapes. Watercolour and gouache media remained popular, while designers continued to apply fine-line ink or pencil to their work for definition and detail.

1   Example of a Gibson Girl illustration by Charles Dana Gibson.

2.   Fashion plate by Paul Iribe from *Les Robes de Paul Poiret*, 1909.

3.   Fashion plate by George Barbier from *Gazette du Bon Ton*, 1922.

A brief history > Art supplies for drawing

1930s

As the exuberances of the 1920s gave way to the sobriety of the 1930s, the fashion silhouette became more elongated, sensual and feminine. Drawing styles reflected the new mood, becoming softer and more textural, while proportions returned to a more realistic interpretation. The surrealist art movement influenced fashion illustration styles during this period, with some notable collaborations between fashion couturier Elsa Schiaparelli and artists such as Salvador Dalí and Christian Bérard, with whom she developed 'shocking pink' for one of her collections.

Drawings took on a more lifelike appearance and the popularity of bias cutting in rayon and silk contributed to a softer, almost slouchy silhouette. The emphasis on back detailing during this time, particularly on dresses, was reflected in the drawings; draping and surface patterns were rendered in inks, watercolours and gouache. Brush strokes became noticeably more enhanced and were used to great effect, in combination with colour washes, to soften the overall look. Women's make-up was becoming more important as new face powders, mascaras and lipstick colours were developed and represented in the drawings, which exuded Hollywood glamour.

1   Fashion plate by Vionnet from the 1930s.

2. Fashion plate by Chanel from the 1930s.

3. Christian Dior's New Look from the 1940s.

1

2

1940s

The austerity of the early 1940s saw another shift in the silhouette, with hemlines shortening, hats taking on a new significance and shoulder pads adding emphasis to a squared-off shoulder-line. Utility dressing and 'make do and mend' became practical necessities. The scarcity of resources during the Second World War was reflected in a more realistic drawing style. Watercolour and gouache were still widely used to render accurate representations of fabrics, colours and prints. Shadow wash effects were sometimes added to enhance the visual composition.

The introduction of Christian Dior's New Look in 1947 changed everything and heralded a new femininity. Drawing styles became more romantic, with bolder, more expressive lines. Designers began to add fabric swatches and positioned the female figure centrally on the page.

B06242
Dior

3

1950s

At the start of the 1950s women continued to wear variations of the New Look, with its emphasis on the small waist and full skirt. Gradually this gave way to different skirt silhouettes, including the new bubble skirt and the leaner, sophisticated pencil skirt. Strapless cocktail dresses were also popular, worn with structured foundation garments to control the silhouette. This style was accented by the new stiletto heel.

Drawings of this period, handled deftly through brush stroke and bold colour wash effects, exuded sophistication and elegance. Watercolour, gouache and inks were all used by designers and illustrators during this time. Towards the end of the 1950s bouffant hairstyles came into fashion and began to appear in sketches.

1

1   Fashion plate of red coat from the 1950s.

2.   Fashion sketch from the 1960s.

1960s

The 1960s gave full expression to youth-orientated pop culture as it swept across the pages of magazines, challenging the status quo and redefining accepted ideals of beauty. Quick-drying, felt-tipped marker pens were introduced during this time and were quickly adopted by designers. The effect on drawings was immediate and lasting as the new pens allowed sketches to take on a more spontaneous and energetic look. The new fashion model was portrayed as youthful and vigorous. Poses changed from being demure and sophisticated to spirited and hedonistic as they projected a new type of freedom for women.

Instead of elegant brush strokes and back washes, drawings took on a more linear, geometric expression, enabled by the new felt-tipped pens. Mixed media drawings appeared, which used combinations of marker pens, pencil, crayon and watercolour.

2

Fashion photography gained in popularity and magazines were increasingly featuring photographs over fashion illustrations. Despite this, drawing styles were still changing and progressively evolved towards decorative and psychedelic expression. Felt-tipped marker pens continued to be used by designers in an expanding range of colours. Drawings became more experimental and the fashion figure began to be rendered in the more abstract form that we recognise today, with elongated arms and legs in sinuous, curved poses.

1

1   Fashion sketch by Louis Dell'Olio, 1973.

2.   Illustration of Montana dress by Richard Rosenfeld, 1983.

1980s–1990s

The 1980s saw a renewed interest in fashion illustration as magazine editors began to commission illustrators rather than photographers for some of their features. It was a deliberate decision in favour of rediscovering the uniquely expressive qualities that a drawing can convey. It also demonstrated a more inclusive approach to the broader visual language of fashion as illustrators continued to experiment with media. While designers were still using felt-tip and marker pens, illustrators rediscovered watercolour and gouache as well as colour pencils, acrylic paints, hard and soft pastel crayons, charcoals and a variety of inks.

The late 1980s saw the introduction of the first CAD (computer-aided design) imaging software programs. These had a major impact on fashion illustration and drawing presentation formats during the 1990s and into the new millennium. At first the new software programs were used to create background effects or simply to apply colour blocking to a drawing. However, as the scope of applications and editing properties became recognised by designers and illustrators, CAD-enhanced illustrations and drawings began to exert their influence and expand the aesthetic view of fashion.

Today, fashion drawings are as diverse as illustrators' imaginations, yet they still serve as a distinctive statement of style.

2

Art supplies for drawing

Setting up your workspace to enable you to draw is a fundamental starting point. You should always begin by considering your light sources: make sure that you can see what you are doing. Some people draw on a flat surface but it is worth considering whether to raise your sketchbook or paper off the table and arrange it into an easel position. This should also free up your arms, which is always the best way to approach drawing. Arranging your art supplies on the same side as your drawing hand will help to reduce unnecessary stretching, and helps avoid simple accidents such as dripping paint on your drawing. Finally, relax and enjoy the experience.

1

Pencils and charcoal

1   Example of working
desk space.

Pencils are among the most versatile and widely used drawing tools for designers and fashion students alike. They are available in a wide range of grades, but most people work within the 2H, H, HB and 2B range. Each grade offers a different density and line quality. The harder grade pencils can be useful for producing fine-detailed line drawings, while the softer grades are well-suited to more expressive sketch drawings and adding tonal values. It's always worth experimenting with pencil drawing, especially when starting out. Pencils are well-suited to most papers and holding positions; they may be sharpened and adjusted and their lines can easily be erased.

Charcoal is useful for fashion life-drawing. Drawing with charcoal is a much looser experience than working with pencil since it offers bolder lines that are not intended to be erased. It is a good media for loosening up and drawing on larger paper sizes. Newsprint is well-suited for charcoal, allowing its deeper tonal values to come through.

Coloured pastels

These broadly describe a family of pastels that includes soft pastels, hard pastels and oil pastels. Made from ground colour pigment combined with gum, soft pastels are available in a variety of vibrant colours and graduated tints. They can sometimes feel slightly crumbly in the hand but are blendable and leave a soft, almost creamy mark on paper. Hard pastels are firmer to the touch. These are suitable for producing broad, flat areas of colour as well as finer lines. Chalk pastels, which are made up of limestone with added pigment, are tonally lighter than pure pigment pastels and require a fixative to prevent smudging. Chalk pastels are sometimes used for fashion life-drawing as an alternative to charcoal and are also available in pencil form. Perhaps less used in fashion, oil pastels do not require a fixative and characteristically produce a thick buttery mark. They can be used on oil painting paper and may be dissolved with turpentine to create softer smudged colours.

Inks

Inks were much used in the early 20th century to produce black or colour drawings and they still offer a distinctive colour media choice. They can be applied with brushes or nibs and are available in a wide range of colours that can be mixed to produce almost any hue. It's important to differentiate between inks that are water-soluble and waterproof. Both can be used to create wash effects, although water-soluble inks tend to sink into the paper and dry to a matt finish. Adding water will dilute the ink further and create lighter tones. Waterproof Indian inks are popular with some fashion illustrators and can be used to create line and wash effects across a variety of paper surfaces.

Paints

The most widely used paints for colour fashion drawings and illustrations are watercolour and gouache, both of which are water-soluble. Watercolour paints are enduringly popular as they offer soft, subtle colour washes and translucent colour effects. Watercolours can be mixed with colour pencil to good effect but should be allowed to dry beforehand. It's best to apply watercolour as a wash without going over it too much as it is not intended to produce an opaque surface. Good-quality watercolour paints have been developed to eliminate hard edges. Gouache is an opaque watercolour paint and is suitable for laying down a flatter, more even and opaque colour. Conversely, it is sometimes watered down but this is not how it should be applied.

Chinagraph pencils

These hard wax pencils are also known as china markers or grease pencils. Originally developed for marking on glossy, non-porous surfaces such as glass, plastic and other glazed surfaces, these versatile pencils also work well on newsprint paper for figurative drawing and sketching. The lines they make are bolder than regular pencils and suitable for mark making. Although mostly available in black they do come in a limited range of colours.

Drawing to communicate your ideas

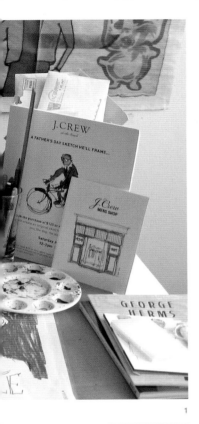

1   The desk of illustrator Richard Haines.

Paper

When choosing paper, there are a number of points to consider. First is to establish the right and wrong side of the paper as this will affect the look of your chosen media. The weight and surface of the paper should also be considered: hot pressed (HP or fine) papers have a smooth, hard surface. This is the smoothest type of surface and is well-suited to pen and ink. Cold pressed (NOT) papers have a slightly textured surface. Rough surface papers take on more of the texture of the paper-making felt and are dried naturally without being pressed. Finally, consider the size of the paper, which will determine issues of scale, and the overall quality: inferior qualities may fade, discolour or easily tear.

Here are some of the main choices of paper for fashion designers and illustrators.

Cartridge papers may have smooth or fine grain finishes and are usually offered for sketch pads in typical sizes from A5 to A3. While the paper is well-suited to pencils, soft pastels and most marker pens it is not ideal for watercolours. If in doubt, ask when you buy the paper or simply experiment with your chosen media on a small piece.

Watercolour papers are designed for applying watercolour and gouache paints. They come in cold pressed and rough surface textures, which makes the paper suitable for holding water. Hot pressed papers are used for lighter watercolour washes and are also excellent for charcoal drawing and pastels.

Layout paper is often used by designers and fashion students for producing line-up sheets or working drafts of technical drawings. This semi-opaque paper is crisp, lightweight and its smooth surface makes it suitable for pencil and pen-and-ink artwork.

Tracing paper is a transparent paper that is designed to be laid over another surface and used for tracing through using all types of pencils and most pens. It is a design-orientated paper and pencil lines can be easily erased.

Newsprint is an inexpensive paper that is suitable for fashion life-drawing and sketching. Available on a roll or in sketch pads, it is a semi-opaque, lightweight paper with an off-white cast and is usually made from recycled fibres. It is well-suited for applying charcoal, pencil and chinagraph.

Multi-media paper (known as vellum in the USA) refers to a good, all-round paper that is suitable for multi-media drawings including pen and ink, marker pens, pencils and oil pastels. These papers are available from most good-quality paper brands.

Marker papers are characterised by their bleed-proof finishes that make them specifically suitable for applying marker pens. They also have a special coating on the reverse side to prevent the markers from soaking through to the next sheet.

Note: North American paper sizes are different from the A4 metric system used throughout the rest of the world. See page 166 for a conversion table.

A brief history > **Art supplies for drawing** > The fashion sketch

The fashion sketch

As we can see from the historical fashion drawings earlier in this chapter, what passes for a fashion sketch has adapted and evolved over time, reflecting an aesthetic statement of style that is broadly aligned to the cultural and social values of the day. Since the 1970s, fashion designers have adopted a wide variety of approaches to the fashion sketch. Individuality is often applauded and encouraged in colleges in the pursuit of creative expression through drawing and, although media choices have expanded and diversified over the years, the fashion sketch remains one of the most alluring aspects of realising a personal drawing style.

An understanding of the human body is integral to fashion sketching, which is usually the process of drawing the clothed figure on a stylised human form. To a lay person, fashion sketches can often appear abstract, energetic or even unfinished, but in fact fashion sketches serve different purposes depending on their intended use. A fashion sketch for a pattern maker would normally require a level of detail and finish that might include line drawings of all the seams,

darts or even topstitching, while a more personal sketch would not necessarily require such detail if its intended purpose was to convey an initial idea or simply explore a silhouette. Experimenting with fashion sketching can help you build confidence and develop your drawing skills. All fashion sketches should aspire towards answering a design problem or a brief. Without this context a fashion sketch might be considered little more than a stylish scribble.

In fashion terms we can talk of figurative sketches that don't need to be realistically proportioned to the human form. Most sketches are drawn with a degree of speed and stylisation that is intended to convey a mood or attitude, beyond visually describing the clothes.

1–2   Sketches by Helena
Kruczynska.

The sketching process

Fashion sketching not only involves the act of drawing an initial idea but also the process of considering and developing the idea across the pages of a sketchbook. It is always best to have an idea of what you want to draw. This may sound obvious, but fashion sketching should be purposeful, not random or too abstract. In many respects a fashion sketch is a problem-solving process, which brings together the visual elements of articulating an idea in its purest form. This can mean recording a sudden idea before it is lost or forgotten, or capturing a moment in time, such as observing a detail on someone's garment.

A fashion sketch should seek to record and make sense of an idea. This is largely achieved with any one or more of three components: establishing the overall silhouette of a garment or outfit; conveying the style lines of a garment such as a princess seam or the positioning of a dart; and representing details on a garment such as a pocket shape, topstitching or embellishment. Some sketches may appear spontaneous or similar to mark making but they should all be linked by a common understanding of the human form and an end use. (Mark making is a general term used to describe a variety of lines and marks that may be applied by different media to enhance or add an expressive quality to a drawing. In fashion drawing it is synonymous with line quality.)

Graphite or drawing pencils are ideal for shading and creating variations of line quality. While this is a good way to get started, it is also well worth developing the confidence to sketch with a pen. Sketching in pen requires a more linear approach to drawing, which can often enhance the clarity of a design idea, and it is no less spontaneous than using pencil, as Lovisa Burfitt's work clearly demonstrates (see pages 44–47).

1

2tone charming top

De denim sting crop

1   Sketches by Jenny Hong.

2   Sketch by Richard Haines.

2

1–2   Sketches by Wei Lu.

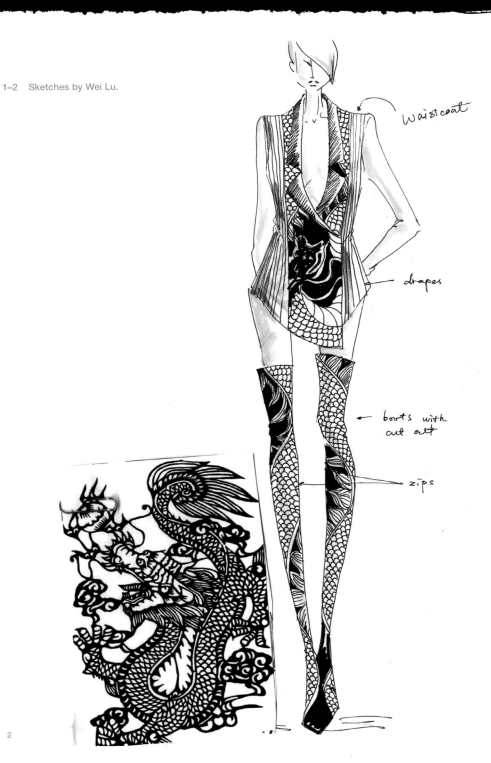

Waistcoat

drapes

boots with
cut out

zips

2

Working drawings

In fashion it is quite usual to produce a series of rough sketches or working drawings in order to arrive at a design or collection proposal. This allows the designer to develop variations on an idea, before making a final decision about a design, whilst at the same time forming part of a critical process of elimination and refinement. The process of reviewing and refining a design involves collating ideas in line-up sheets. These represent drawings of outfits (not individual garments), which are visually presented on the human figure as a coherent statement for a collection proposal. Line-up sheets are more practical than inspiration sketches or rough sketches and are generally clearer to understand on the page. Their primary purpose is to assist with visual range planning and the commercial requirements of formulating ready-to-wear clothing ranges. Consequently, they have no real basis in haute couture or bridal wear, which is more about representing the individual.

MISC

(3)

- archeology
  fragments → fragmented → deconstructed
  └ broken down beat
- near east → Iraq / Iran / Afghanistan / Persia
- soft, dry...

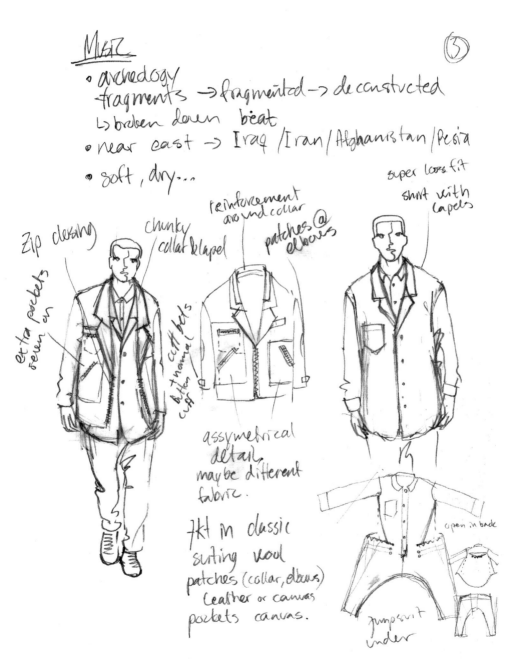

super loose fit
shirt with
lapels

Zip closing

chunky
collar & lapel

reinforcement
around collar

patches @
elbows

extra pockets
sewn on

cuff bets
button normal
cuff

assymetrical
detail,
maybe different
fabric.

Jkt in classic
suiting wool
patches (collar, elbows)
leather or canvas
pockets canvas.

open in back

jumpsuit
under

2

une about
is me need
o think more.

folds
continu-
ed and
let to
hang
loose, rather than
being cut off by
panel, not sure
how this will work with, skirt,
dress, like detail being at back.
On't like bottom panel, makes it too
hard, want more organic +
slight bulbous shap
lso folds going into
sleeve

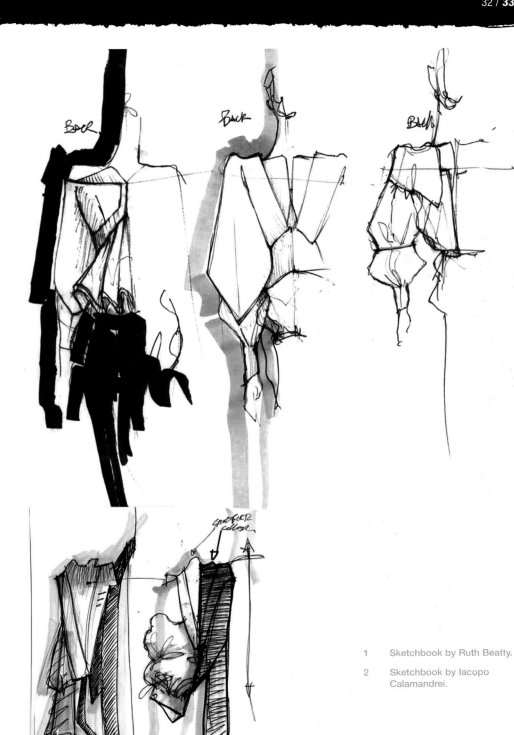

1   Sketchbook by Ruth Beatty.

2   Sketchbook by Iacopo
         Calamandrei.

1   Sketchbook by Iacopo
     Calamandrei.

2   Sketchbook by Ruth Beatty.

1

6
change skirt
+ jacket collar

change
trousers +
pocket

Sketchbooks

Sketchbooks are the repository of a fashion designer's ideas, observations and thoughts. Whilst there is no template for the perfect sketchbook (and they are not solely the preserve of fashion designers), a good fashion sketchbook should enable the designer to progressively record and document a series of ideas and inspirations through related visual and written material accumulated over time.

All sketchbooks evolve in response to changing influences and circumstances. The true value of a sketchbook is in how the designer uses it to pause and reflect on their work in a meaningful way in order to continue to the next stage of the design journey. It can sometimes be difficult to fully comprehend this when starting out; there may be a temptation to fill up the opening pages with lots of secondary images but this will not lead to a personal sketchbook unless it starts to take on the personality of the user, rather like a personal diary or journal. A sketchbook should become as individual as your fingerprint and provide you with a growing resource from which ideas and concepts can be explored and

developed without feeling self-conscious. Sketchbooks also enable you to explore and develop your own drawing style; the book will build up over time and its resource value will increase. One of the most useful aspects of a sketchbook is its portable nature, allowing you to carry it around and enter quick thumbnail sketches or observational drawings.

Most fashion student sketchbooks are A4 size. However, there is no fixed rule on this as some students successfully work with A3-size sketchbooks. Sometimes working across a landscape A3 format can be useful for sketching A4-size fashion figures and developing preliminary line-ups. The smaller A5 pocket-size sketchbooks can be useful for discreetly carrying around; they also work well as fabric swatch books and for entering additional thumbnail sketches. (See page 166 for the North American equivalents to A3 and A4.)

1–2   Sketches by Helena
        Kruczynska.

Working drawings > **Sketchbooks** > Elmaz Hüseyin

1

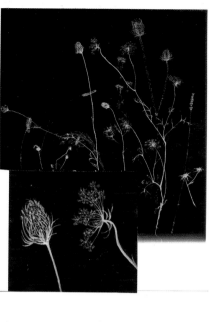

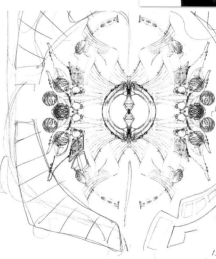

#5 passi

#4 passi

#3 passi

#2 passi

#1 passi

#5 trama 8 capi
ottene
4# trama 8 capi
Oro L + rupple
3# trama 8 capi

oro L + mauve
2# trama 8 capi

oro L + arancio
1#
trama 8capi
oro L + verde

JC4   raso 5/cambiato effetto con
raso turco

JC 3 #2   10 passi al cm   trama a 8 capi
raso 5   oro + verde
raso turco

JC 3 #1   12/13 passi al cm   trama a 4 capi
fondo Raso 5   oro + verde
raso turco

JC2   12 passi al cm   trama a 4 capi
Fondo natté   oro + verde
Fondo rasoturco

JC1

oro e verde   fondo
                                  tela

trama viscosa 1 capo

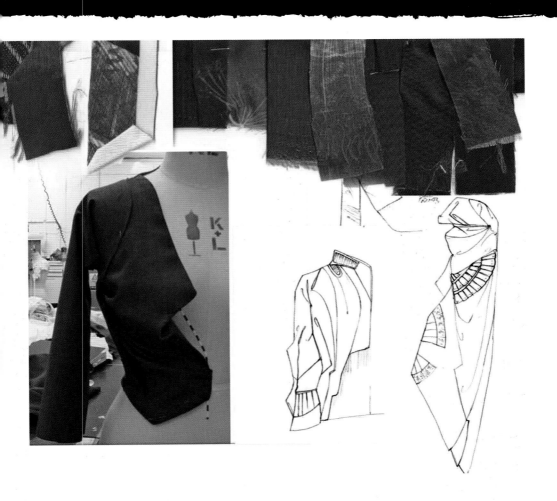

1 Sketchbook by
Iacopo Calamandrei.

OUTFIT ONE SHIRT/SINGLE ALL-IN-ONE.....

(PRINT ON ALL-IN-ONE)

OUTFIT TWO ALL-IN-ONE WITH CHIFFON OVERLAY.....

OUTFIT THREE DRESS.....

OUTFIT FOUR JERSEY HOODED DRESS.....

CHIFFON SHIRT AND SLIM TROUSER.....

1–2   Sketches by Janine Cloke.

Elmaz Hüseyin, fashion designer

Please describe your current job
I am a freelance design consultant,
working within the industry and
related areas. I am also involved in a
project at a more fundamental level,
creating a pilot fashion design
module for schoolchildren who
are interested in design.

**What was your career path
to your current job?**
I have basically been practising as
a design professional since I left
college, first with my own line and
later choosing to immerse myself in
the mass market. I worked full-time
in the industry up until last year when
devastation hit with the credit crunch
and many designers were made
redundant overnight. Consulting is
what many of us have opted to do
until the industry recovers – or
possibly permanently.

**What makes a good
fashion sketch?**
Attitude, line, clarity – I like to
start with a great hairstyle and
face. Attention to detail, such as
accessories, can accentuate the vibe
you're trying to communicate. It's
important for me to be excited by
what I see and I should be able to
get 'lost' in them.

**How would you describe your
drawing style?**
Realistic but not realistic, sometimes
caricaturist (which design sketches
can be), comical and whimsical,
exciting, usually with movement
and flow in the lines.

**What type of media do you
like to use when you draw?**
I almost always start with pencil on
layout paper. I rough out some good
poses either from life, from my head
or magazines. Then I love to 'clean'
them up by loosely tracing them with
Indian ink and a dip pen. This forces
you to draw pretty quickly and gives
you clean, meaningful lines with
varying widths – I love using this
method. Then I work by lightly filling
in colour using pastels. I also make
copies and use colour pencils,
Pantone and highlight with gouache
if necessary.

Who or what inspires you?
Normal people inspire me... I could
be sitting on a train and notice
something amazing about a girl or
boy who's done something cool with
their uniform or something. I can be
inspired by an old lady who wears
her hat a certain way. I was once
inspired by a NY street vendor who,
amazingly, had his teeth set with
emeralds and rubies to look like dice.

**Do you have any advice for
someone starting out in the
fashion industry?**
Be patient, there is so much to learn
and college can only prepare you
with the basics. Something new
(both good and bad) is always lurking
around every corner. Follow your gut
feelings and keep your standards
high, particularly if you choose the
mass-market route where small,
not-quite-right things can become
big ones in production. Believe in
yourself, otherwise no one will
believe in you.

1

2

1–3   All sketches by Elmaz
      Hüseyin.

DH 8010
Lace
Swagger.

Lovisa Burfitt, fashion designer and illustrator

Please describe your current job
I'm working on drawings for Bloomingdales, which they are using in their various kinds of communications for their department stores.

What artistic training have you had?
I studied design and drawing at Beckmans School of Fashion, and then went on to study at the Royal College Of Art, Stockholm.

How would you describe your fashion drawing style?
Adrenalin kick-style, quick and clean and rough.

What type of media do you like to use?
Ink feather, pen and brush using ink are my favourites, and my style is pretty much that. I mix materials depending on mood, such as felt pen, a lot of coloured pencils, a variety of ball point pens, crayons, basic pencils and so on.

What makes a great fashion drawing?
When you sort of feel the quick move of the brush or pencil, understanding the anatomy instantly in your stomach by the first look.

What advice do you have for a student to develop their drawing skills?
To really practise your eyes and hands to draw what you see, and to practise drawing anatomy by nude studies, over and over again, until it comes automatically like walking or riding a bicycle.

What or who inspires you?
Music influences me a lot, it gives soundtracks and moods to my pictures.

1–2   Illustrations by Lovisa Burfitt.

CAN'T GET OUT of THIS MOOD

Elmaz Hüseyin > **Lovisa Burfitt**

Lovisa Burfitt, fashion designer and illustrator

1

3

1–3 Illustrations by Lovisa
Burfitt.

2

1   Illustration by
       Holly Mae Gooch.

*'I like the body. I like to design everything to do
with the body.'*

Gianni Versace

Having looked at the purpose and evolution of fashion
drawing, both as a statement of style and a means of
communicating an idea or design, it is important to
apply a greater understanding of the fashion figure to the
development of a contemporary and personal drawing style.

In this chapter we will look in more detail at the fashion
figure and consider the value of working with a life model to
gain primary drawing perspectives. We will also examine the
differences between observational drawings of the human
figure and the idealised forms that characterise the fashion
figure for men and women. Different approaches between
drawing men and women are compared and contrasted
as we consider how to proportion the human body to a
fashion scale. We look at the value of working with poses to
communicate an attitude and create the desired look, along
with associated gestural attributes, which are characteristic
of figurative fashion drawing. The use of drawing media and
line quality will also be presented and considered in relation
to the evolving fashion figure.

Drawing to communicate your ideas > **The fashion figure** > Technical drawings

Understanding fashion proportions

1   Sketch by Helena
     Kruczynska.

2   Nine-heads figure template
     by Helena Kruczynska.

The proportions of a fashion figure are often exaggerated and stylised, particularly for womenswear drawings. This can sometimes be slightly confusing to the untrained eye but in fashion terms it represents a statement of an ideal rather than an actual body shape. This ideal is then aligned to a contemporary look that is viewed through the visual lens of fashion.

Since the late 1960s and 1970s exaggerated proportions have generally prevailed and continue to exert an artistic influence over most fashion drawings. Most standing fashion figures are proportioned between nine and ten heads in height (if the figure's head is arranged vertically on the page alongside the complete standing figure). Most of the additional height is gained through the legs, with some added to the neck and a little added to the torso above the natural waist. Most women in the real world stand around 5ft 5in or 5ft 6in, but a fashion figure needs to project greater height in order to better show off the clothes and communicate the look to an audience, usually through exaggerated gestural poses. Of course, a woman who might be 5ft 2in could be proportioned the same as a woman standing 5ft 10in but for fashion purposes neither would offer the desired ideal proportions for communicating the look. When drawing the fashion figure the look might refer to the prevailing styles of the season, such as the position of the fashion waist, or it may be an exploration of voluminous or contoured clothing styles with reference to influences from a particularly favoured model or celebrity.

There are fundamental differences between the fashion proportions for drawing men and women. Women's fashion proportions are mostly concerned with extending height through the legs and neck, with the resulting drawings taking on a sinuous and gently curved appearance. For men the drawing approach is altogether more angular. (See Drawing men on page 70.)

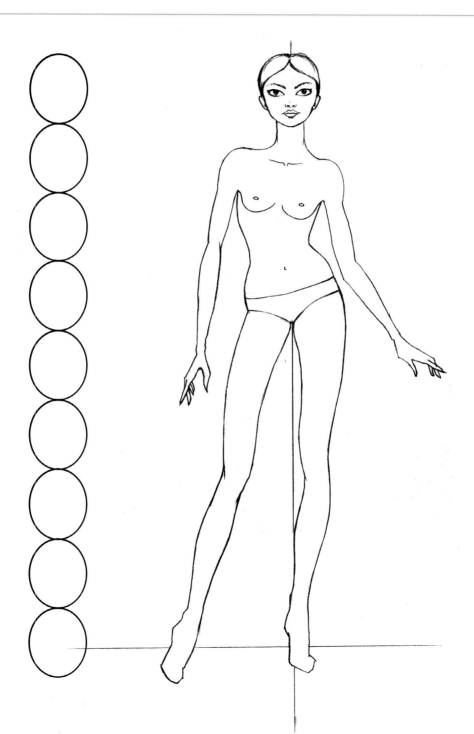

Understanding fashion proportions > Drawing from life

Drawing from life

Drawing from life, which is an excellent way to develop and refine your drawing skills, involves observational drawing of real-life male or female figures. It is important to consider the appropriate art materials and media, such as charcoal, pen or pencil, as well as paper type and the eventual scale of work. Working to larger sizes, such as A3 or A2, is often best when starting out or simply for loosening up (see page 166 for more on paper sizes).

Drawing is a process that can be improved and enhanced with regular practice and life drawing offers the particular opportunity of developing and improving hand-to-eye coordination. This is essentially about trusting yourself to spend more time looking at the figure in front of you, rather than by glancing at the figure then looking at the emerging drawing itself and drawing from memory. This is a common mistake among life-drawing students.

It is very important to study the figure before you start to draw. Try to make sure that you are in a good viewing position and then analyse the pose. If the figure is standing it is essential to establish which leg is taking most or all of the weight; this will critically determine the stability of the pose in relation to what is called the 'balance line'. The balance line is an imaginary line that drops from the base of the centre of the neck down to the floor at the position of the foot. It can be drawn on the paper and used as a guide to ensure that the figure remains standing without 'tipping over' on the page. As a general rule, the leg that is supporting the weight of the pose, which should always be drawn before the other leg, will curve down to the floor and should join up with the balance line at the outside edge of the foot.

The principle of the balance line applies to all standing fashion poses including those simulating a walking pose. It is also applicable to menswear although men's poses are generally made less dramatic and gestural than for women's fashion drawing.

Studying the pose first also allows time to evaluate distinctions between the 'actual' figure and the expression of an 'ideal' fashion figure for womenswear or menswear. Proportions in fashion drawing represent an ideal, so it follows that the life figure does not need to be drawn as an exact representation. This requires interpretative visualisation, which is an essential release for fashion drawing.

1

3

1–3 A series of observational life drawings by Helena Kruczynska.

Creating poses

1   Line drawing of pose by
    Holly Mae Gooch.

Fashion drawings are frequently characterised by gesture and movement, both of which are ideally suited to exploration through drawing the fashion figure from life. Part of a fashion drawing's allure is its seemingly effortless style, which is sometimes the result of a careful selection of lines and what is left to the imagination of the viewer. In this regard it is important to note the value of line quality in the fashion-drawing process.

Line quality describes the varieties of drawn lines or marks that have their own inherent characteristics depending on the media that is used, the paper quality, the speed at which the line is made and even the angle of the pen or pencil as it moves along the surface of the paper. Distinct from adding tone and shading techniques, the use of line to convey essential information is integral to most fashion drawings.

Some of the most expressive and visually engaging fashion poses are the result of linear drawings, where selective line quality is used to maximum effect. An understanding of fashion proportions and the standing balance line is essential as a building block for more gestural poses, which instil movement and personality into a fashion drawing. In addition to studying poses from life, it is also possible to develop poses by tracing over figurative photographs in magazines, but this needs to be approached with care: consider the image only as a starting point. Fashion is, after all, a human activity so it follows that developing and creating studied poses is a useful exercise and will aid the development of templates or croquis for future use.

It should be possible to use a pose more than once and for a template figure to present different design ideas. While the pose should be relevant to the context of the clothing (for example, it would make little sense to draw a sporty pose for a wedding dress or an evening gown), creating the pose is much more about the body underneath. Look for movement lines that run through the body – not the outline of the figure – noting the intersections of the pose at the bust, waist and hip positions. The leg supporting the weight must be grounded, but the other limbs can be modified or adapted to enhance gestural qualities. In this way, the resulting fashion poses can exaggerate the 'actual' to project a more expressive 'ideal'.

Croquis
Croquis is a French word for a sketch. In fashion terms, it describes a linear drawing of a figure that may be used as a template over which to trace and draw a design or garment. Figurative fashion templates or croquis are typically exaggerated to a nine- or ten-heads proportion.

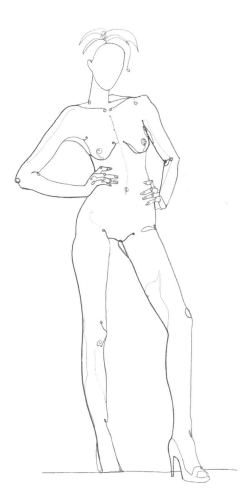

1

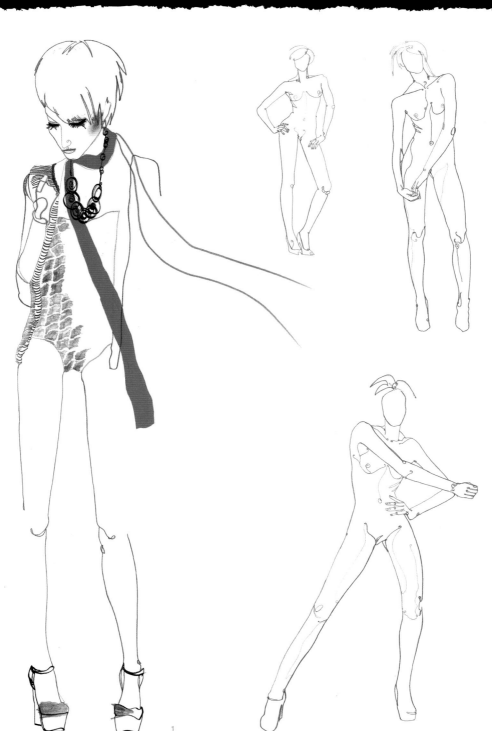

1–4 Selection of drawings by
Holly Mae Gooch. The
figures in 2 and 4 are line
drawings of different poses;
1 and 3 show studies of
poses in a fashion context.

4

3

Fashion heads, faces and hair

1   Developing a study of
    a fashion face by
    Holly Mae Gooch.

Fashion heads, facial features and hairstyles are worthy of special consideration in fashion drawing; they can convey a multitude of essential style and gender information. The very personal and unique attributes that a face can contribute to a drawing are worth exploring through practice and exercises. Much like the evolution of fashion drawing itself, the 'ideal' face changes over time and takes on many guises. Make-up trends continue to have a direct influence on contemporary fashion faces and it is always useful to collect magazine tear sheets from which to study and evaluate different faces and proportions.

1

1   Study of a fashion face by
     Holly Mae Gooch.

1

2

Faces

Although faces can be drawn in the linear style that is so often used in fashion, they can also lend themselves to applications of tone and shade. Structurally, the forward-facing head is oval in shape for women – much like an egg shape – and should be horizontally intersected at mid-point to position the eyes. The mouth is usually arranged halfway between the eyes and the base of the chin. The mouth could be considered in two parts with its upper and lower lips. The upper lip should include an 'M' shape definition. The nose may either be represented with dots for the nostrils above the top lip of the mouth or with an added off-centre vertical line from the front of the face as if to indicate a shadow. Noses are rarely given any prominence in fashion faces as the eyes and lips become the main features.

Eyes lend themselves to thicker lines and smudging effects but take care not to overwork them. Eye shadow can be added for greater effect and to provide colour. Lashes should also be considered and can have a dramatic effect on the overall visual appeal of the drawing.

The ears may be discreetly added at the side of the head starting at eye level and ending just above the nostrils; they can be useful for displaying earrings, if appropriate.

3

4

Hair

The hair should be carefully considered as this can have a transforming effect on the appearance of the fashion head. Again, collect tear sheets from magazines in order to build up a visual file of hairstyles as it can be quite challenging to imagine them without a reference point and of course, hairstyles for women vary enormously. If it is visible the hairline should be drawn around a quarter of the way down from the top of the oval shape of the head. Line, shade and colour can all be added according to the style requirements and context.

1–2 Study of lips and eyes by Holly Mae Gooch.

3–4 Two hairstyle studies by Holly Mae Gooch, showing the drawing development.

Arms, hands, legs and feet

1–3   Studies of hands and arms
      by Holly Mae Gooch.

When drawing a fashion figure it is important to consider the hands, arms, legs and feet in relation to the pose and gestural qualities. The standing figure needs to be drawn with due consideration of the balance line, so that the leg that supports the weight of the figure is drawn at a gentle curve down to the floor, with the outside edge of the foot placed where it meets the balance line. Correctly positioning the leg that supports the weight of the figure is critical in determining the credibility of the pose; consider this in relation to the upper body position and the placement of the arms, which can often counterbalance the exaggerated form of the legs.

Although it is helpful to understand anatomy and muscle tone in relation to figure drawing, for fashion drawings the arm muscles are not emphasised on women. Instead, the lines of the female figure should remain gently curved and drawn as a continuous line wherever possible. Longer lines are a discernible characteristic of fashion drawing and help to convey a sense of style and confidence.

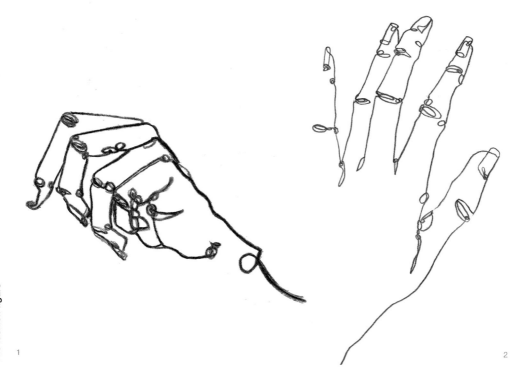

Drawing arms and hands

When drawing an arm, consider it in three parts: the upper arm, the elbow and the lower arm. The upper arm is attached to the shoulder from which it may pivot depending on the angle of the torso. It has a smooth, gently tapering upper section that reaches down to the elbow position. The elbow can be drawn in a variety of ways depending on whether the arm is viewed from the front, in which case a discreet line is usually sufficient; or from the side, when its flexible, more 'pointed' character defines the angle of the lower arm. This part of the arm tapers more visibly to where it joins the hand. Women's wrists should be narrow just above the hand and may sometimes be adorned with a bracelet or bangle depending on the desired look.

In drawing terms, the hands have two main parts: the front or back of the palm and the fingers and thumb. Both parts may be elongated to offer the fashion figure a range of gestures and actions, which will all enhance the drawing. Consider the angle of the lower arm when drawing the hand. Fingernails may be included but knuckles are not usually emphasised: too much detail on a hand can make it look wrinkled. You could also try drawing the hand resting on the hip with the fingers hidden from view.

3

1

2

Feet

The feet are usually drawn in a simplified way that mostly assumes a shoe line. When starting out it is helpful to practise sketching bare feet, but the foot will usually be hidden from view within a shoe, which can be drawn in a huge variety of styles. The overall look will be determined by the angle of the foot and whether or not the shoe has a heel.

Legs

As fashion drawing is largely concerned with presenting an interpretation of an ideal figure rather than realistic proportions, so it follows that drawing the legs is an exercise in artistic licence. Fashion legs are routinely extended in the upper leg and thigh, and below the knee to where the ankle meets the foot. Referring to the principle of head heights in fashion, half the total height of the female figure (i.e. four head heights) is taken up by the legs from below the crotch position.

When drawing a leg, approach it as three parts: the upper leg or thigh; the knee; and the lower leg or calf, which joins the foot. The upper leg should be gently rounded and taper to the knee position; this can be sketched out as a circle but on a finished drawing is usually indicated with a slightly extended line from one side of the upper leg to indicate its forward position. It is not emphasised but marks the position from which the lower leg starts and gently curves down to the narrowest part of the leg just above the ankle.

1–2 Legs and shoes by
Holly Mae Gooch.

3 'Talons' illustration by
Lovisa Burfitt.

3

Drawing men

1   Linear menswear drawings
     by Fiona Hillhouse.

2   Menswear illustration by
     Thomas Rothery.

It has already been noted that fashion drawing is largely concerned with presenting an ideal figure rather than an actual body shape and this principle also applies to drawing men. Physical gender differences must be taken into account and are usually emphasised in order to assert a position of masculinity, depending on the desired age and attitude to be conveyed. In fashion drawing terms, men can cover a wider age range than most fashion drawings of women, rather like male models whose careers tend to extend beyond their female counterparts. The male figure can be elongated to nine or ten heads in height; when compared to the female figure the torso is longer and correspondingly the overall leg length is slightly shorter, particularly the lower leg from below the knee. Perhaps the most striking difference, however, is the emphasis of muscle tone, which is applied more readily to the male figure. When drawing male and female fashion figures on the same page, the male figure should stand slightly taller than the female, or at the same height.

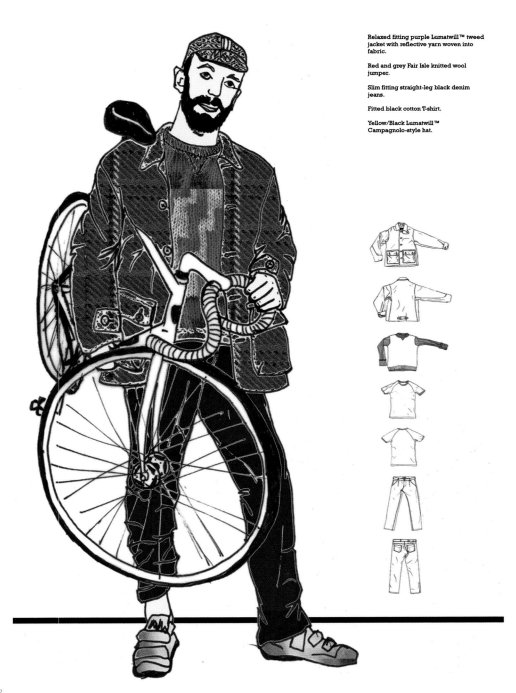

Relaxed fitting purple Lumatwill™ tweed jacket with reflective yarn woven into fabric.

Red and grey Fair Isle knitted wool jumper.

Slim fitting straight-leg black denim jeans.

Fitted black cotton T-shirt.

Yellow/Black Lumatwill™ Campagnolo-style hat.

Arms, hands, legs and feet > **Drawing men** > Howard Tangye

The male fashion figure

Starting from the head and working down to the feet, let's consider the male figure in more detail. First the head shape is drawn differently. Instead of an oval egg shape the head usually appears more angular and chiselled with a squared-off jawline. A jaw dimple is sometimes added. Eyes are positioned at mid-point. Eyebrows add definition and can be emphasised as a horizontal line, but not the upper lid of the eye as this might appear like make-up. The mouth is drawn wider and straighter than for women; ears can be added to the side of the head from eye level to just above the nostril level. The neck is not used to gain height and is drawn to a more natural length than for women, appearing thicker and less curved as it joins up with the shoulder.

The upper torso of the male figure is drawn as the widest part of the body before the addition of the arms, and tapers slightly to the waist. The waist size is much thicker than for women but the line from the waist to the hips is almost parallel and should always appear trim, as the hips are not emphasised on a man and should look noticeably narrower than the chest width. Stomach muscles may be defined where it is appropriate to the look. The arms and shoulders add further width to the male silhouette and are thicker and more muscular than for women. Wrists and hands can also be drawn thicker; the fingers are blunter and less tapered than for women. It is interesting to note the different approaches to male and female gestures. Arms are generally drawn

closer to the body unless specifically engaged in an activity such as holding a ball or an umbrella. The hands are not used as expressively as they are for women, much beyond gripping objects or being positioned in pockets. Overall, fashion poses for men are typically less dramatic and certainly less fluid than for women.

1

2

Poses

The principle of the balance line applies equally to standing poses for men as it does for women. Men's legs are not drawn with the same degree of curve and are correspondingly thicker and more muscular in character. The knees can be drawn more prominently than for women while feet are drawn larger and more angular. Men can be drawn in activity poses such as walking, riding a bike or climbing and can also look credible when they are cropped, appearing to be closer to the viewer, which also adds to their physical presence.

Drawing from life provides a valuable means of learning to draw men by directly observing and studying male proportions and credible masculine poses. Magazine images can also be useful for referencing hairstyles and a range of movements. Longer lines are generally preferred in fashion drawings and while this is also true for drawing men, the lines tend to be straighter. They can almost appear joined up, like a series of interconnecting points, or with inflections, which interrupt a line that might otherwise look too graceful and feminine.

1   Illustration by Aaron Lee Cooper.

2   Line drawing by Holly Mae Gooch.

3–4   Sketches by Richard Haines.

3

4

Howard Tangye, fashion illustrator and senior lecturer at Central Saint Martins

Please describe your current job and your career path

I am the senior lecturer for womenswear in the Fashion and Textiles School at Central Saint Martins College of Art and Design. This involves working with large groups of very talented people who have varying points of view and tastes. Being part of student development in art and design and their related skills is incredibly interesting and inspiring. My responsibility is to keep the students inspired and challenge their ability; to set project briefs and encourage a dialogue, so that there is always something new and in-depth coming through.

I have worked professionally as a designer and an illustrator. But my teaching position is now full-time so I have to maintain a discipline of sorts to practise my own personal work alongside that. It works because I love both equally.

How would you describe your drawing style?

I think my drawing style has evolved with, and been affected by, the changes in my life. As a child I drew naturally, in a naive way, from my imagination. I loved colouring books and illustrated reading books at school. Then I was very fortunate to be taught by Elizabeth Suter as a student at Central Saint Martins.

She taught how to look properly, to be aware of the body, in its movement, proportion, the bones, details, using the layout of the page, use of media and so on. This affected me in the most profound way. Drawing was an elective subject in the design school. When working in the drawing studio we always drew from life models of various shapes and sizes. The quality of the teaching was evident in the results and the standards of both design and drawing in the school. All the tutors were able to draw. The philosophy of the school then, as now, was to enable the student to develop their confidence, to be themselves.

1–4   A vibrant use of colour is characteristic of Howard Tangye's work (figures 3 and 4 shown overleaf).

1

I have two different approaches to drawing: working from the model, looking and feeling the line or texture; and from my imagination, usually in small and intimate sketchbooks. The two come together at some point.

What type of media do you like to use when you draw?

I like to work with mixed media on paper: oil sticks, pastels, graphite pencils, inks, gouache, brushes and pens. The quality of paper is very important to me, both in terms of the texture and also its ability to hold all the above and I like to see the paper through the media. I also like to see what happens to the media afterwards when it is viewed under a magnifying glass. It is a whole other world of marks and colour not seen when just viewed with the naked eye. It's magic.

What common mistakes do students make when drawing?

The most common mistakes students make when drawing are that they do not look at the figure closely and they don't concentrate. Both are essential.

What elements make up a visually engaging composition?

The elements that help make up a visually engaging composition are the use of the negative space and how the figure is placed on the page. Traditional Japanese artists are masters of it.

What or who inspires you to draw?

Drawing is hard work. It is demanding but I am inspired to draw the figure by people who have caught my eye, by the way they look, the way they move, their posture and so on. Everybody has individual qualities that are attractive but certain temperaments can be the key. It's a two-way thing: the sitter has to work at it too.

Drawing men > Howard Tangye

Howard Tangye, fashion illustrator and senior lecturer at Central Saint Martins

4

1   Students working with
           Lectra software program.

*'Even when I work with computers, with high technology,
I always try to put in the touch of the hand.'*

Issey Miyake

This chapter considers the importance of understanding
how to draw individual garments as part of the fashion
drawing process. In contrast to the more stylised approach
used to draw the fashion figure, this chapter introduces the
realistic proportions and techniques for drawing flats and
specifications, or specs as they are more commonly known.

We discuss the role of computers in fashion drawing and
their application to a variety of presentation enhancements
and visual formats. This includes an introduction to dedicated
software programs that continue to be developed and refined
to meet the needs of the fashion industry. Visual examples
distinguish between the different presentation requirements
of technical drawings for fashion. Finally, there is an insightful
interview with the director of a design consultancy that
produces specs for a number of international clients.

Understanding garments

1   Specification sheet by
     Elmaz Hüseyin.

The ability to demonstrate an understanding of individual garments
is fundamental to fashion design and covers an area that we might
broadly describe as 'flats' and 'specs'. While both terms are widely
used in design education and across the ready-to-wear fashion
industry, there are some important differences between them.

A flat is an individual garment, or series of garments, drawn in the
flat to represent a three-dimensional form as if it was laid down and
viewed from above. Front and back views are usual, although side
views can also be included depending on the visual information to
be conveyed. Flats are essentially linear drawings, which may be
enhanced for presentation purposes.

A spec (short for specification) is a more technically orientated and
exacting presentation of an individual garment, drawn in a precise
linear style to convey detailed technical information. The drawing is
presented on a specification sheet, an internal document that a
company uses for manufacturing purposes, which contains
essential technical information such as the assembly processes,
fabric, trimmings and costings.

RV7096

```
- SNAPS =   B-075 CONTRAST TO MATCH "B"
- ZIPPERS = #5 DTM MOULDED PLASTIC TO MATCH "A"
- ZIPPER PULLS = DTM LC-242 TO MATCH "A"
- UNDERSIDE OF COLLAR = DTM "A"
- FILLING IS POLYESTER
```

**RV7096 SAMPLE COLOUR:-
- A= WHITE
- B= GO-GO LIME
- C= HIKE ORANGE**

B-075 top snap

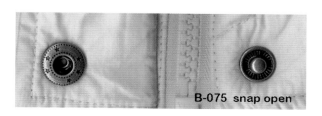

B-075 snap open

PG#:	PG7099
DESCRIPTION:	NYLON SHELL
CONTENT:	shell = 100% nylon
	lining = 100% nylon
GRAMS:	filling = 100% polyester

STITCH THROUGH
ALL LAYERS
OF COLLAR

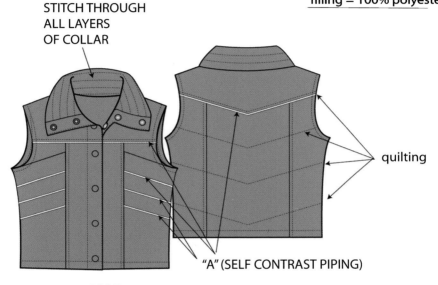

quilting

"A" (SELF CONTRAST PIPING)

RV7097

- SNAPS = B-075 DTM
- MAIN BODY & LINING = DTM
- CONTRAST SELF PIPING = "A"
- FILLING IS POLYESTER

**RV7097 SAMPLE COLOUR:-

- GO-GO LIME

- "A" = WHITE**

Garment characteristics

There are different approaches to drawing flats and specs, yet each requires a fashion student or designer to demonstrate their knowledge and understanding of an individual garment. Flats and specs are therefore not as much concerned with the overall look, as a figurative drawing might be, but rather with the detail and characteristics of the garment. These characteristics could be defined through a series of three main visualisation processes. The first is an understanding of the overall silhouette and proportion of the garment. Flats and specs are drawn with much more proportional accuracy than equivalent figurative illustrations, so instead of a nine- or ten-heads figure, a more realistic eight-heads figure is used.

The second requirement of flats and specs is to document the style lines. This includes drawing all seams and darts that shape the garment and any additional features such as gathers or pleats. All style lines can be drawn using linear techniques that shouldn't rely on shading, colour or tone. It is also important to include back views of all style lines to demonstrate a full understanding of the garment. Style lines such as ruffles, added fullness or pleating variations can be drawn in a variety of ways, all of which are achieved through drawing technique and practice. Look at examples of other flats or specs to increase your own knowledge and understanding. As your level of technical knowledge increases, and your practical skills improve through pattern making and

draping in the studio, so too will your ability to draw garments efficiently and effectively. In short, a student who does not understand the basic elements of fit and shape will be less able to draw competent flats that are indicative of a fully resolved garment design in two dimensions. It is always a good idea to draw a flat or spec as if you had to give it to someone to cut or drape without you there to explain it.

The third visualisation process that makes up a flat or spec is the application of detail lines. These include topstitching and other visual surface applications, such as a patch pocket, for example, which does not affect the fit of the garment but is integral to its final presentation.

1–2 A selection of flats by
SnapFashun, a specialist
company that provides
vector graphics templates.

Drawing fashion flats

1 Presentation of flats
  on design board by
  Emma Frame.

2 Flats by Nuttawan
  Ness Kraikhajornkiti.

The approach to drawing fashion flats is generally more varied and less formal than drawing a corresponding specification drawing. It is important to consider what the purpose of the flat will be. This might sound rather obvious, but flats can be applied to several different end uses. The first of these might be to demonstrate a full understanding of a design that is presented as an artistic illustration or figurative drawing. It can sometimes be appropriate to include a flat alongside a figurative drawing in order to better explain the design. However, this has to be considered in relation to the compositional value of the drawing; for some illustrations it may be unsuitable. Arranging flats on a separate presentation board is another option.

Another purpose of flats is to demonstrate range planning skills. In this regard flats serve an important function: they are extremely useful for breaking down a collection into its component parts. This can be by product, such as a visual analysis of all the skirts or tops within a collection; or by theme, such as grouping together all garments that make up a travel-themed capsule within a larger seasonal collection. In this way flats provide a distinct and additional presentation value to a designer's portfolio.

Although flats can be drawn with the aid of software programs, when starting out they are best drawn by hand. Use a pencil or pen to trace over a realistically proportioned eight-heads template/croquis figure. You can either refer to an existing figure or create your own by tracing over a standing pose in a magazine and refining the pose to a simple outline of realistic proportions. Use the same template or croquis figure for all your flats within the same presentation to achieve visual consistency and scale. Hand-drawn flats can also be drawn larger than their intended scale and reduced down to the required size. This is a good way to get started and allows for an enhanced level of detailing, such as topstitching. While flats should be drawn with a high level of clarity, there are a number of views on whether a flat should be drawn symmetrically or not. It is good to practise drawing a symmetrical garment by hand: draw half the garment and fold it over to trace off the other half. However, perfect symmetry is not essential: one sleeve could be folded at the elbow, for example, to show more detail or simply to enhance the visual effect. There are limits to taking a more relaxed approach when drawing flats but by adding a few drape lines or using a variety of line thicknesses, flats can appear less 'flat' and begin to take on more three-dimensional qualities.

Digital techniques
In considering the commercial context of flats and their presentation value to buyers or as part of a fashion designer's portfolio, it is possible to accommodate enhancements such as colour and line quality. Increasingly, presentation flats are being coloured up using software programs such as Illustrator or Lectra's Kaledo design software.

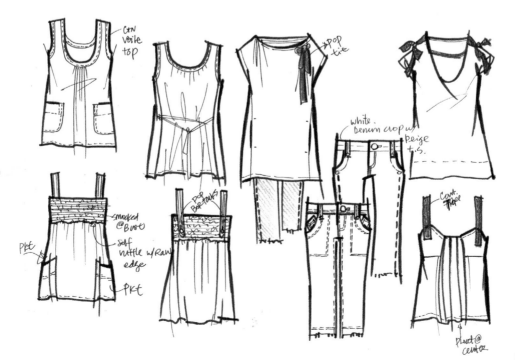

crisp ctn
nylon
popover.

Striped
sheer
top.

stv
twill
uop

knit top
w/ off shldr
slvs w/ woven
tabs 1 Binding

light ctn
waffle
hoody

woven top Applid pkts.

WOVEN
HEM w/ knit
jersey skirt w/
tunnel @ WAIST.

1–2 Hand-drawn flats by
      Jenny Hong.

3–4 Computer-aided flats by
      Nuttawan Ness
      Kraikhajornkiti.

ctn
voile
top

pop
tie

white.
denim crop w/
beige
t.s.

smocked
@ Bust

self
ruffle w/ Raw
edge

pkt

pkt

pop
bar tacks

cont.
tape

plact @
center

Drawing technical specifications

1   Specification sheet by
    Elmaz Hüseyin.

2   Spec drawing by
    Aaron Lee Cooper.

Technical specifications or specs (also referred to as technical drawings or schematic drawings) are approached in a more formal fashion than flats. This is because a specification drawing has an industrial context that is closely linked to a manufacturing specification or cutting sheet instruction.

Technical specifications contain the visual information required for the manufacture of an individual garment in relation to its associated unit costs, such as all trimmings and design details, which might include labels or an embroidered logo. They are not used for range planning or to visualise an outfit unless, for example, the garment is made up of two parts for manufacturing purposes, such as a coat with a detachable hood. Specification drawings are always produced after a design has been formulated. They are prepared in readiness for a production run through a factory unit or for a 'sealed sample' for assembly on a production line. Technical specifications should always be drawn in a clear and linear style: they need to be accurate and clear enough in their detail for a factory manager or garment technologist to understand them and to provide sufficient information for a sample machinist to be able to assemble the garment without additional instruction.

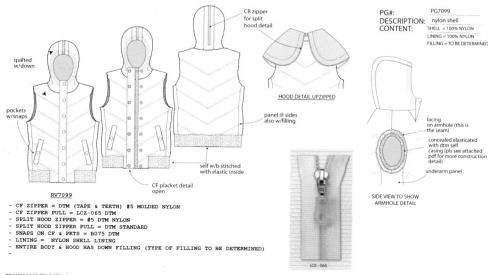

quilted
w/down

pockets
w/snaps

CB zipper
for split
hood detail

HOOD DETAIL UPZIPPED

panel @ sides
also w/filling

self w/b stitched
with elastic inside

CF placket detail
open

RV7099

PG#:   PG7099
DESCRIPTION: nylon shell
CONTENT: SHELL = 100% NYLON
              LINING = 100% NYLON
              FILLING = TO BE DETERMINED

facing
on armhole (this is
the seam)

concealed elasticated
with dtm self
casing (pls see attached
pdf for more construction
detail)

underarm panel

SIDE VIEW TO SHOW
ARMHOLE DETAIL

LCZ-065

- CF ZIPPER = DTM (TAPE & TEETH) #5 MOLDED NYLON
- CF ZIPPER PULL = LCZ-065 DTM
- SPLIT HOOD ZIPPER = #5 DTM NYLON
- SPLIT HOOD ZIPPER PULL = DTM STANDARD
- SNAPS ON CF & PKTS = B075 DTM
- LINING = NYLON SHELL LINING
- ENTIRE BODY & HOOD HAS DOWN FILLING (TYPE OF FILLING TO BE DETERMINED)
-

The ability to draw an accurate fashion spec requires a high level of technical knowledge combined with a steady hand. Most fashion students will not be at this advanced level when starting out. Moreover, not all fashion designers will be required to produce a factory spec. However, in practice, fashion students and designers should be able to understand them and produce a detailed line drawing of a garment when working with a pattern maker. Specification drawings serve an important function in identifying and eliminating potential faults before production. As such, they are increasingly being drawn with the aid of computers using a variety of CAD/CAM programs, signalling a move towards a more integrated design and manufacture approach.

Vector graphics and bitmaps

1–2 Vector graphic fashion illustrations by Nuttawan Ness Kraikhajornkiti.

Digital graphics media first emerged in the 1980s. Desktop scanners and more efficient graphics tablets soon followed, enabling designers to digitise hand-drawn artwork for the first time. The development of digital drawing and image-editing software during the late 1980s heralded the arrival of early vector graphics and bitmaps. In simple terms, vector graphics are geometric formations such as lines, points and curves, which are based on mathematical equations to represent a digital image. They produce clear lines that are suitable for drawing flats or specs; linear quality is not reduced when scaled up or down in size. Bitmaps are the data structure represented by a grid of pixels that makes up a digital image, measured as dots per inch (dpi). Pixels are the building blocks of bitmap images such as digital photographs and scanned images. The more pixels an image has per unit, the better the quality of the image for colour and resolution. Bitmaps are also known as raster graphics and are stored in various image files such as JPEGs or TIFFs.

Since their early application, graphics software programs have steadily developed and expanded into a variety of sophisticated user platforms, which can be used for enhancing fashion presentations.

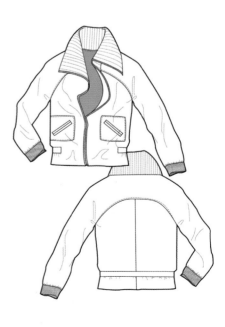

Techniques include digital drawing, colouring, rendering and image editing for visual formats. Foremost among the available software are Adobe Illustrator and Photoshop, which have become industry standards. Photoshop is a graphics editing program that is primarily geared towards photo manipulation. Illustrator is a vector-based drawing program, originally developed for the Apple Macintosh in the mid-1980s. Today it has evolved into a sophisticated digital drawing tool that allows for the conversion of bitmap imagery into vector art. Illustrator's versatility makes it well-suited for creating composite illustrations and layouts, which are excellent for drawing and presenting flats. Illustrator can also incorporate images and text with vector graphics to enhance presentations. Other software programs of note are CorelDRAW, a Windows-based vector graphics program and its raster image creation and editing counterpart, Corel PHOTO-PAINT. Macromedia Freehand is another powerful vector graphics tool that is orientated towards the desktop publishing market and now owned by Adobe.

Drawing technical specifications > **Vector graphics and bitmaps** > Tomek Sowacki

Fashion software

Specialist IT providers have developed dedicated fashion software applications. For example, French company Lectra has developed Kaledo, a Windows-based fashion design software package. SnapFashun in the United States has developed a CAD system to serve the fashion industry, which includes an extensive library of fashion flats and garment details that digitally 'snap' together (see page 82). Intended to assist busy designers working in industry or fashion students with creating and drawing their flats, SnapFashun's vector graphics templates are compatible with Adobe Illustrator.

As well as their labour-saving capabilities, these graphics applications and CAD solutions offer extended opportunities for designers to modify their ideas and working processes. The ability to draw by hand will always be relevant in fashion and should be practised and maintained. But increasingly, as we shall see later, developments in fashion illustration are witnessing a synergy between hand-drawing styles and digital enhancements.

2

3

1

4

5

6

1–7 A selection of screen
images showing Kaledo,
a fashion design software
program from French
company Lectra.

7

Drawing technical specifications > **Vector graphics and bitmaps** > Tomek Sowacki

Tomek Sowacki, design director

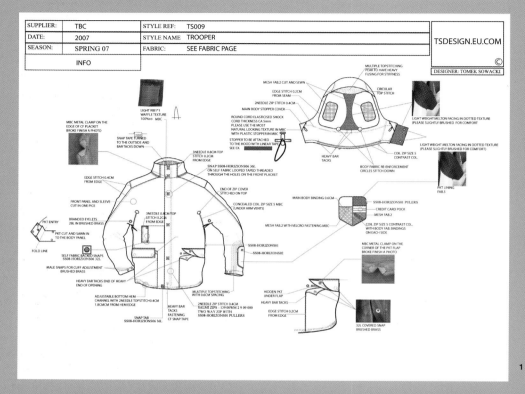

SUPPLIER:	TBC	STYLE REF:	TS009		
DATE:	2007	STYLE NAME	TROOPER		TSDESIGN.EU.COM
SEASON:	SPRING 07	FABRIC:	SEE FABRIC PAGE		
	INFO				DESIGNER: TOMEK SOWACKI

1

Please describe your current job

I work and manage a freelance design consultancy agency: <www.tsdesign.eu.com> It consists of a network of experienced and dedicated designers; we take on a variety of projects from clients in the fashion and textile sector. Our work includes fashion design, graphic design and logo design.

What was your career path to your current job?

After completing my MA at Central Saint Martins, I started to work for sport-specific brands such as Adidas, Puma and Tommy Hilfiger Sports, as well as lifestyle brands such as Levis and Rip Curl. I also had my own brand, Yucon, which was successful but we ran out of funding. With my overall experience as designer and manager I decided that I prefer freelancing or self-employment so my current situation, managing my own freelance business, suits me perfectly.

How would you describe your artwork?

Carefully thought through and usually rich in detail.

How important are computers to what you draw?

Computers are vital to my work as they allow me to be clear and specific in detail; any alterations can be done then and there. They make it easier to share the information between me, my clients and factories; I think they are essential to any business these days and I would be lost without them.

What type of software do you need to be able to use?

My favourite is Illustrator on Mac as it is fantastic for technical drawings and it links up with the whole Adobe Suite such as Photoshop and others.

What makes a good fashion flat or technical drawing?

I would say a clear one: when you are able to give the drawing to production and the person 'reading' the drawing is able to execute the design according to the information given without having to ask any further questions. Good drawings are important as they can save time and not halter the progress.

What are your favourite garments or subjects to draw?

I really enjoy designing outerwear as I think these garments in particular require you to think jointly about function, style and technical aspects due to the different end use (such as who will wear it, where, when, in what weather and so on). This allows me to indulge in the details of the garment, internal as well as external, to create maximum style and functionality.

Do you have any advice for someone starting out in the fashion industry?

Make sure you love it, persevere in the industry and find a career path that suits you!

1–2   Design and corresponding spec sheet by Tomek Sowacki.

Vector graphics and bitmaps > Tomek Sowacki

'*I like light, colour, luminosity. I like things full of colour and vibrant.*'

Oscar de la Renta

In this chapter we look at the influence of colour in fashion drawing by considering how it affects design presentations and media choices for artwork. Colour theory is also introduced and evaluated in relation to hand-rendering techniques and the development of computer-aided drawings and associated colour schemes. The particular role of mixed media and collage for fashion is considered, with a variety of supporting visuals that provide an introduction to the wide range of media choices that have become integrated into contemporary fashion artwork. We also look at the application of colour to different fabrics, textures and prints. The chapter ends with an engaging interview with a fashion design illustrator who has collaborated with a number of international fashion houses to produce colour prints and textiles for their seasonal collections.

1   Illustration by Wendy Plovmand.

1

Colour for fashion

Colour media for fashion has evolved over the years and it has had a direct influence upon the visual style and presentation of fashion drawings. The introduction of marker pens in the 1960s confirmed a particularly significant shift towards faster and more responsive media, which were specifically design-orientated rather than historically rooted in a tradition of artist materials. Marker pens still exert a powerful influence over fashion sketching styles and drawing techniques. Today, however, the range of colour media that is available to fashion designers and design students must also be considered in the context of computer-aided design software.

Let's start by briefly considering what colour represents from a fashion perspective. When most of us look at images of clothes in a magazine or see a fashion window display we are immediately drawn to the colour of the clothing and accessories. Moreover, fashion collections are routinely designed and visually merchandised into seasonal colour themes. Colour is a fundamental, powerful force in the design process, from fabric selection through to the completion of a design. It is also a vital component in fashion that can have a transforming effect upon audience perceptions and reactions. Some designers such as Matthew Williamson or Manish Arora are well-known for their engaging use of colour, while other designers use colour to make a statement or add specific pieces to their collections.

Colour can also be expressed through embroidery, appliqué and a variety of trimmings such as zips and buttons, as well as colour dyes and printed textile designs. Fashion labels such as Basso Brooke, Cacharel and Eley Kishimoto are all known for their use of colour through printed textiles. The selection and application of colour is a decision driven by emotion but it can have a transforming effect on a design. Consider, for example, a dress design conceived and drawn in beige and then the same design presented in red. We would respond to them differently, even though the dress would be in the same style. Such is the emotive power of colour.

Despite personal preferences there is really no such thing as a bad colour. It is an artistic or design decision to select a colour and apply it to a design, choosing whether or not to combine it with another colour. The appearance of a colour is dependent on light: it will take on a different appearance when viewed under different optical conditions. The multitude of shades, tones and hues that are available today through synthetic or natural processes can be broadly identified within a colour wheel classification.

1   Manish Arora S/S08.
     Catwalking.com.

2   Matthew Williamson S/S09.
     Catwalking.com.

2

1

The colour wheel

The colour wheel visually represents the basic principles of colour theory. The wheel is divided into three categories: primary, secondary and tertiary. The three primary colours are red, yellow and blue. These may be considered as the foundation colours since they are used to create all other colours and are equidistant on the colour wheel. The combination of two primary colours creates three secondary colours: orange, green and violet, which are also equidistant on the colour wheel. The six tertiary colours are made by combining a primary and an adjacent secondary colour. These equidistant colours make up red-orange, red-violet, yellow-green, yellow-orange, blue-green and blue-violet. Colours may also be divided into cool and warm categories: cool colours are classified as green, blue and violet. Warm colours are classified as red, orange and yellow. When mixing colours, a tint of a colour is made by adding white, while a darker shade is made by adding black.

Colour schemes

When working with colour media it is worth remembering that there are three basic colour schemes. The first is a monochromatic colour scheme, in which a single colour is used with its various tints and shades. The second is an analogous colour scheme. This is when a colour such as red is used in combination with its adjacent hues such as red-orange and red-violet. The third type of colour scheme is made up of a variety of contrasting colours and includes the complementary scheme. This is when two hues that are opposite each other on the colour wheel are used together. For example, red and green are opposites, and are considered complementary colours when used together as they make each other appear brighter and more intense. Other colour combinations exist such as 'split complementary', which is a derivation of the complementary scheme and uses three colours comprising any hue and the two adjacent to its complement. This could be, for example, a combination of red, yellow-green and blue-green.

1   The colour wheel.

2   Examples of different colour schemes.

2

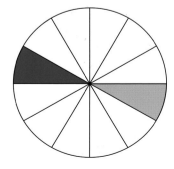

Complementary

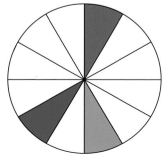

Split complementary

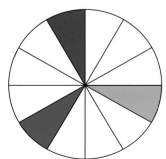

Triads

1

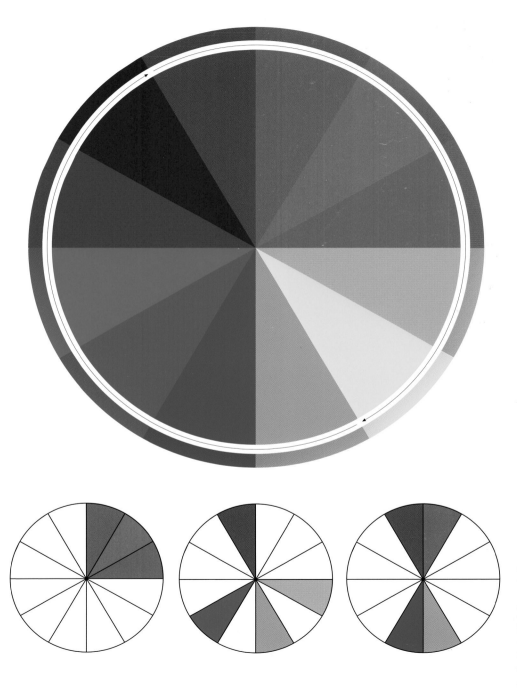

Analogous

Mutual complements

Double complements

Colour forecasting

Selecting colours – or, more specifically, the right colours for a particular season – is crucial in the fashion industry and can mean the difference between success and failure in terms of a label's image and sales. Fashion designers will often visit their suppliers to discuss colours for the coming season and will work closely with their textile partners to develop 'lab dips' and 'strike-offs' for printed textiles. Additionally, the global fashion industry is served by a network of trend and fashion forecasting companies that provide detailed colour analysis, colour direction and market-trend research for fashion and interiors up to two years in advance of the selling season. Companies such as Trendstop, Peclers, Li Edelkoort for Trend Union and Promostyl, among others, are well-respected authorities on colour, each producing a variety of specialist reports for their fashion clients. They also employ fashion-orientated illustrators who contribute to their publications with hand-drawn illustrations alongside CAD artwork and colour presentation flats.

1–2

1–8   Colour forecasting and catwalk trend images from Trendstop.

Lab dips

A process whereby a fabric swatch is test dyed to meet an exact colour standard. Lab dips are reviewed in a light box under controlled lighting conditions and may be analysed with a spectrometer.

Strike-offs

A strike-off is a small run of screen-printed fabric, which is used to test the integrity of the screen for accuracy and colour trueness. It also refers to fabric that is printed in new colours or on new grounds with existing screens before a production run.

DAFFODIL 14-0850 TPX

4

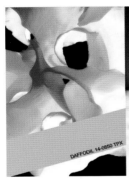

FLAMINGO 16-1450 TPX

5–6

CANTELOUPE 15-1239 TPX

MELLOW YELLOW 12-0720 TPX

7–8

CADMIUM YELLOW 15-1054 TPX

Colour for fashion > Fabric rendering

Fabric rendering

1   Drawing by Howard Tangye.

The ability to draw fabric convincingly is a useful skill for any designer or fashion illustrator; it is often taught to fashion students as a means of broadening their drawing skills and their knowledge of fabrics. The process is usually referred to as fabric rendering. Of course, there are many different types of fabrics to draw and while some might have surface texture and pattern, others do not. Evaluate a fabric's inherent characteristics, properties and its weight in order to establish whether the fabric will drape over the body convincingly or whether it might present itself as more structured and firm to the touch. A designer sketch or linear fashion drawing should communicate a convincing understanding of the chosen fabric or fabrics. For more artistic illustrations the rendering process can be somewhat looser and more interpretative.

The best way to start is by copying a real fabric swatch. Much like drawing from life, this entails keen observation and evaluation of the fabric before starting the drawing process. Selection of appropriate media is critical: prepare a variety of colour media, which can be used in combination. To start with it is best to draw to the same scale as the fabric. The scale will later have to be considered when it is applied to a figurative drawing, but by establishing how to imitate the appearance of the fabric and what media to use in the first instance, the process of rendering the scale of the fabric to a fashion figure won't seem so daunting. To simplify things it can help to categorise fabrics into a select number of groups such as woollen and textured fabrics, shiny fabrics, sheer fabrics, knits, patterns and prints. It is worth attempting each group of fabrics, since they are all likely to be drawn at some time.

1

Textured fabrics

Woollens and textured fabrics form a good starting point. This category might include wool flannels, meltons, gabardine, suitings, wool challis and crêpes as well as camel hairs, Shetland wools and tweeds. Typically opaque, these sorts of fabrics are used in autumn/winter collections. Marker pens or gouache can be used to lay down the base colour as a wash effect, while colour pencil or a slightly dry brush can be added to create the desired texture or brushed appearance. Tweeds can be drawn with the addition of cross hatching and flecks; try pronounced twill weaves with a sharp pencil line. Wool plaids are typically built up in layers, starting with a base colour created as a wash followed by weft and warp colour bands. Darker layers are usually added later with finer lines towards the end, especially for the lightest colour, drawn in pencil.

1

Shiny fabrics

Rendering shiny fabrics for the first time can often be more challenging than opaque fabrics and, since they reflect light, typically need to be considered in relation to a light source. Surfaces might be smooth or have a moiré effect. Shiny fabrics such as taffetas, charmeuse and satins should be drawn with a combination of dark, medium and light tonal values. Sometimes it is effective to leave white space to indicate where the light has the most pronounced effect on the surface of the fabric. This applies to pale or white fabrics, such as those used for evening or bridal wear; these fabrics have tonal variations. Marker pens, watercolour paints and Indian inks are all useful media for rendering shiny fabrics and can be used in combination with colour pencil for accents.

2

Sheer fabrics

Sheer fabrics, such as chiffons, georgettes and fine voiles, are characterised by their transparency and parts of the body may be visible beneath the fabric. Rendering these fabrics presents unique challenges as there can be many values of a colour depending on whether the fabric is layered or worn over the skin. Their general appearance should be light of touch without hard edges, drawn using media such as marker pens, blendable pastel chalks or watercolour. Colour pencils or chalks can be combined with other media to create the effect of transparency. Hems and seams should be understated.

Knitted fabrics

Knitted fabrics can be drawn to convey surface structure and texture and are typically defined by the inclusion of a ribbed edge or cable effect. A base colour wash in gouache or marker pen is effective and works well with the addition of pencil lines to define the knitted surface of the fabric. A dry brush effect can also be applied to represent courser yarns. This group also includes jersey knits, which can take on a more fluid appearance; this can be rendered in a tonal wash.

1–2   Drawing by Claire Bushey, shown with corresponding fabrics.

3–4   Drawings by Fiona Hillhouse.

5   Drawings by Miyuki Kitahara.

Colour for fashion > **Fabric rendering** > Collage and mixed media

Patterns and prints

Rendering fashion fabrics with patterns and prints offers scope to use a variety of colour media, depending on the desired effect and base fabric quality. Prints can add a dramatic visual look when applied to a fashion drawing and need to be studied carefully. The most important aspects to consider are the repetition and scale of the print. Some prints are designed for borders, such as hems, while placement prints typically adorn the fronts of T-shirts. Most fashion prints are repeat prints so applying them to the scale of a human figure becomes a necessary consideration. Rendering a print on to a figurative drawing or illustration will require you to consider line quality in relation to an understanding of the garment. It is important that the print is drawn to look like it is printed on the surface of a fabric that has folds, drapes and is sewn together with seams. With this in mind, shading techniques can also be applied.

1–2   Illustrations by Wendy Plovmand.

3   Drawing by Howard Tangye.

3

Collage and mixed media

1–2   Mixed media illustrations by
      Holly Mae Gooch.

3–4   Collage compositions by
      Wendy Plovmand.

Derived from the French word *coller*, meaning to glue, collage was originally taken up by artists to describe the technique and process of assembling different forms to create a new work. In fashion design collage is synonymous with the term 'mixed media' and is used to describe a hybrid approach to creating artworks that might include a variety of papers, photographs, fabrics, buttons, ribbons, threads and other objects to either replace or supplement the drawing process. While collage was traditionally carried out by hand, with techniques such as cutting and pasting, it has now become widely embraced by fashion illustrators through digital formats such as Photoshop, with some exciting and diverse results that continue to push the boundaries of fashion illustration and presentation formats.

What makes collage and mixed media artworks for fashion so popular and visually engaging is their diversity, allowing you to work outside the usual conventions of art supplies and drawing media. Hand-made collages also encompass tactile and textural qualities that make the final drawings almost three-dimensional in character. Some even incorporate stitch. Collage and mixed media artworks for fashion often transcend and mutate the notion of the fashion ideal to something that is more abstract than a single drawing or photograph could communicate on its own.

Developing collage or mixed media illustrations for fashion is a creative process that allows for a high level of artistic expression. As with most approaches to creating artworks it is best practised and refined over time, but is underpinned by an inventive curiosity, a love of technique and good compositional skills. One might even be tempted to draw parallels between the appropriation of found objects to create fashion artwork and the notion of fashion continually reinventing itself. In this sense collage and mixed media for fashion take on a more poignant context.

1

2

3

Din modeguide
Efterår 2007

4

Fabric rendering > Collage and mixed media > Digital colouring and rendering

Digital colouring and rendering

1–3 Digital colour illustrations by
Wendy Plovmand (1 and 3)
and Aaron Lee Cooper (2).

Continuing developments in digital graphics software has enabled fashion illustration to be redefined alongside more traditional hand-drawing techniques. Today many designers and fashion illustrators combine both formats for a contemporary drawing style.

Digital colouring, rendering and collage describe a variety of bitmap (raster) applications and vector graphics. These include scanning and retouching hand-drawn illustrations as well as creating digital freehand drawings using either a mouse or a graphics tablet and pen. These processes can be applied to a fashion illustration or used for creating colour-enhanced presentation flats.

Scanning a hand-drawn sketch or illustration is an effective means of creating a digital fashion image for editing and retouching. You may wish to resize or enhance the artwork for digital storage, using a number of artwork effects from the software's graphics toolbox, which are represented by icons such as a pen tool, brush tool, scale tool, eraser and stroke, and colour fill boxes.

3

Digital colour

Understanding colour schemes is essential for working with digital colour swatches. In this regard there are two main colour models to consider: RGB and CMYK. RGB is a colour model in which the additive primary colours of red, green and blue light are added together to reproduce a broad spectrum of colours. The main purpose of the RGB colour model is the representation and display of images in electronic systems such as scanners, digital cameras and computers. RGB is generally faster to work with than CMYK and well-suited to screen display. However, RGB images need to be converted to CMYK for commercial printing purposes. CMYK is a subtractive colour model used in colour printing, which applies cyan, magenta, yellow and key (black) to the printed surface.

Also worth a mention is Pantone, a US-based global colour authority that serves the fashion industry and other sectors with a comprehensive colour classification and matching system. The Pantone Color Matching System is a standardised colour reproduction service that enables designers,

printers and manufacturers to all work together to exact colour specifications across Pantone's wide range of spot colours. Pantone's spot colours cannot be simulated with CMYK but require base pigments, including white and black, to be mixed in specified amounts.

Today, all digital graphics software offers a comprehensive range of colours, textures, gradients and patterns that can be applied to a drawing and edited through the use of palettes and layers. Palettes display editing and monitoring options such as working with RGB or CMYK colour. Layers allow users to separate different elements of an image so that each layer can be saved and edited independently. This is particularly useful when building up an image and adding elements such as colour or texture. In addition, specific fabrics, patterns and surface textures can be scanned from original sources and added to palettes or taken from computer-generated fabrics.

1   CMYK colour model.

2   RGB colour model.

3–4   Digital colour flats by
       Witney Cramer.

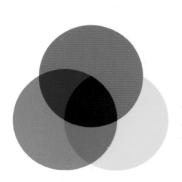

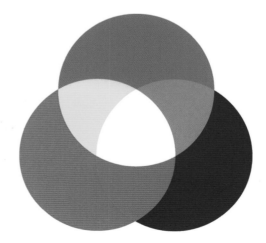

Soft Plush with Stripe

3 1/2"

3 1/2"

TOTAL REPEAT=7"

3

Black with Blue's Clue

Black with Twilight Grey

Dark Mud with Amethystine

CHUNKY MULTI COLORED STRIPE
3GG

TAUPE PEAKS

WHALEBONE

CORN CHIP

SMOGGY HEATHER

AMETHYSTINE

PLUM SAUCE

GOLDEN TROPHY

DARK MUD

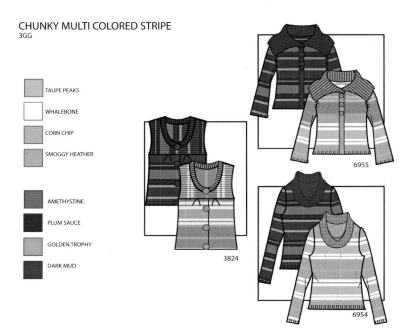

6955

3824

6954

4

Collage and mixed media > Digital colouring and rendering > Petra Börner

Petra Börner, fashion illustrator

1

Please outline your current job and your career path

Although I trained and worked many years in fashion, design and illustration, commissions now involve clients within interior design, publishing, editorial, packaging and advertising. Current projects include limited edition packaging design for Swedish Liljeholmens, collaborating with Heal's for their 2010 bicentenary campaign, designing crockery for a Japanese client and creating embroideries for Jonathan Adler Interiors. I have been a visiting lecturer at Central Saint Martins College of Art and Design since 2001, mainly in fashion illustration.

How would you describe your drawing style?

I work with references or themes in simple compositions, using mixed techniques such as drawing, collage, sewing and painting. My cut paper compositions have sometimes been described as looking like wood-cuts and a significant Scandinavian characteristic is distinguishable in my work.

I try not to determine the outcome before the work is created, leaving the process of making art spontaneous and fun. This enjoyment is most apparent when working from a life model (essentially with some really good music).

Through my work I aim to express an identifiable individual rhythm or handwriting, which is perhaps plain or elegant in its interpretation of chosen subjects or scenes.

Subject matters vary from working to set commissions with defined starting points, to artwork that derives from a simple curiosity to find a way to draw something new or specific. In my opinion, natural references or photography (a 'raw' base) lend themselves better to visual interpretation than a cleverly designed or functional object (such as a mobile phone), which has already reached a solution. However, there are exceptions, as I'm fond of drawing cars and robots.

Tell me about your collaborations with fashion houses

My main experience of fashion design came through running my own business and in 2004, when I decided to be a full-time illustrator, this experience gave me vital confidence in collaborations with fashion houses.

One of my first commissions in fashion was with Clements-Ribeiro for Cacharel on the A/W06 collection. They acquired a dozen of my artworks to be transformed into fashion prints and I remember being delighted by seeing my work projected as the backdrop of the catwalk in Paris. I enjoy being involved in varied types of collaborations and I find fashion fits perfectly well with advertising jobs, interior design or book-cover illustrations. The process of these collaborations is much the same; sometimes the starting point is specified, sometimes open-ended, but with fashion I consider colours, placement, the look of the repeat and the scale of the design carefully.

1   Yellow field print, an original artwork for Cacharel, by Petra Börner.

2   Embroidered artwork by Petra Börner.

Digital colouring and rendering > **Petra Börner**

Petra Börner, fashion illustrator

What type of colour media do you like to use in your artwork?

I work in a variety of media, but at most starting points, thoughts of colour and composition are central. For example, if I am creating an illustration in cut paper I tend to select the colours of the paper as my starting point and from there imagine the development of the structure. I also use paint, ink, thread and, at times, digital manipulation to modify colours according to the needs at hand. The beauty of colours created or assembled by hand seems superior and more refined than any digital work I create. The fine-tuning of achieving harmony between colours is an intuitive process to me.

How important is colour in your work?

Colours are central to all my work and an artwork disappoints if colours of an illustration or print are manipulated after the artwork has been created. This is an element that can be a concern in collaborations with clients, who often work towards strict colour structures and have to consider the blend with other products. I enjoy the element and possibilities given by working with colours and seldom rely solely on contrasts between black and white. I often involve tones or shades of the same hue within an artwork to create depth or as a way to play with the focal point. To me, the mastering of colour is the more challenging part of illustration and art, more than the composition.

What advice do you have for fashion students who want to create colour artwork?

It's a good idea to create basic colour compositions and analyse the result. I would try to find an enjoyable and useful method to work with (mixing paint, using DIY paint cards, cutting paper, stickers, wood, metal, photography, stitching, knitting) and then create interesting, attractive, perhaps unusual combinations. As with drawing, repetition is key to define the colours that represent your identity.

Who or what inspires you?

I'm attracted to work that combines charm, spontaneity, skill and confidence; art that feels part of a circumstance and is clearly representing the artist's self, with an effortless vitality achieved only by the urge of repetition through time.

1–4   Cocoa bean dress for Cacharel A/W06 (1) and pieces from Cacharel's S/S07 collection (2, 3 and 4), all featuring Petra Börner's print designs.

2

3

4

1   Illustration by Luis Tinoco.

*'To create something exceptional, your mindset must
be relentlessly focused on the smallest detail.'*

Giorgio Armani

In this chapter the important differences and distinctions
that coexist between fashion presentation formats are
considered. Building on an understanding of the fashion
figure and the role of technical drawings for fashion, this
chapter explores how they may be grouped together as
part of a coherent presentation. The particular perspective
of fashion illustration is considered in relation to other
artwork formats, while a range of artwork boards, sometimes
ambiguous in nature, are visually presented and explained.
We look at the growing influence of digital presentation
platforms, including websites and blogs. The chapter is
richly supplemented by interviews with three inspirational
illustrators who each apply their different styles and talents
to contemporary fashion illustration. Their distinctive media
choices and eclectic styles are testimony to the diverse
language used by fashion drawing today.

1

Fashion illustration

1–3 Fashion illustrations by
Timothy Lee (1) and Tahsin
Osman (2–3).

Fashion illustration describes a particular approach to fashion drawing that exemplifies artistic expression and stylisation of the human form. On the whole it is concerned not so much with an accurate representation of the garment or outfit, but with communicating the allure or attitude of the design. In this regard fashion illustration may be considered as being distinct from fashion sketching. We may also refer to fashion illustrators as distinct from fashion designers, although both work in complementary ways and the production of fashion artwork is common to both practices.

Some of the most successful fashion illustrators have had little or no design training and therefore do not involve themselves in the complexities of pattern cutting or the manufacture of a garment. This is not their function and it does not restrict an illustrator; they have no need to add every seam, dart and tuck to their final illustrations. In fact, such detailed information can sometimes make a fashion illustration appear static or overworked, especially if the details are already clarified in a designer's flat drawing.

Fashion illustration is about capturing the mood, the spirit and the essence of a design. Some of the most effective fashion illustrations can appear almost effortless, inviting the viewer to imagine what lies beneath the surface or to form personal interpretations. Of course, illustrations are not effortless and developing an illustration is a process in itself, one that requires practice, visualisation and experimentation. Personal illustration styles evolve over time.

3

Composition and layout

Composition in fashion illustration refers to the arrangement of the visual elements within its defined dimensions, and the relationship between these elements. As there is such variety in fashion illustration, applying fixed rules to composition is not really appropriate. However, there are some underlying principles that should be considered by fashion students – these may also be regarded as intuitive.

The relationship between the elements can be classified by what is referred to as the 'positive image' and the 'negative space'. The positive image refers directly to the subject, usually the human figure in a fashion illustration, while negative space refers to the space around and between the subjects. The positive image and negative space are equally important in determining a visually engaging composition.

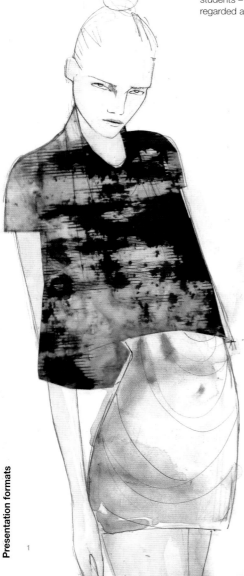

The layout of a successful fashion illustration has considered placement in order to achieve the desired effect or visual impact. This is usually aimed at capturing the viewer's attention and directing their eye over the illustration. Before the arrival of digital media this was achieved through a manual process of rough draft planning and gradually layering up the composed illustration. Today, the ability to work with separate layers for digital images has facilitated the process and made it much more versatile. Once in digital form, illustrations may be edited and formatted to fit a particular presentation or printing requirement. Whichever route you take, whether it is hand-rendered or digital, planning and composing your illustration is always important and you should consider the illustration's purpose – for presentation or inclusion within a portfolio.

1   Fashion illustrations by Anna Walker.

Presentation boards

Most fashion students will be familiar with the term presentation boards as they are frequently used when working on projects and preparing a portfolio. The term is also used in the fashion industry to refer to a variety of boards that communicate and sell ideas or designs for commercial objectives.

Presentation boards are primarily concerned with presenting ideas and designs to a defined audience with an appropriate level of clarity, visual flair and professionalism. They serve different complementary functions and, when considered within a project or specific presentation, they should be visually linked. This might include, for example, working across a template and colour code style and using the same board dimensions within a presentation.

Strong compositional skills, and the ability to clearly communicate information, are a distinct advantage when preparing a presentation board. Presentation boards that are executed with clarity also convey a student or designer's organisational skills (and this is important for working in fashion). Presentation boards should not blur into each other or repeat the same information as the viewer or audience will quickly lose interest or become confused.

1

Bicycool: Autumn/Winter 2009

T ⊙ ☐
By Thomas Rothery

2

Bicycool: Autumn/Winter 2009

Outfit 1   Outfit 2

1. Grey cotton "button-back" shirt, wool and lammerel(ette) tweed trousers and scarf.

2. White (plain-back) cotton shirt, yellow cotton t-shirt, black cotton denim jeans, and waterproof nylon poncho.

T ⊙ ☐
By Thomas Rothery

Bicycool: Autumn/Winter 2009

T ⊙ ☐
By Thomas Rothery

1   Illustration boards by Chi Hu.

2   Illustration board (top), design board (middle) and flats presentation board (bottom) by Thomas Rothery.

Mood board

One of the most frequently used boards, and one that most fashion students are introduced to first, is a mood board. As its name suggests, the purpose of this board is to set the mood or tone for the design boards or project work that follows. The process of preparing a mood board also enables a designer to collect visual information from a variety of sources and to organise their inspirations and ideas into a composed visual display. These boards can vary considerably from intense photomontages or composite collages to rather spare visual compositions that convey an ethereal quality. Some mood boards are tactile, others may be digitally formatted. Depending on the guidance provided by tutors or professors, either type may be acceptable but it is still important that the board is planned, arranged and edited into a coherent visual composition.

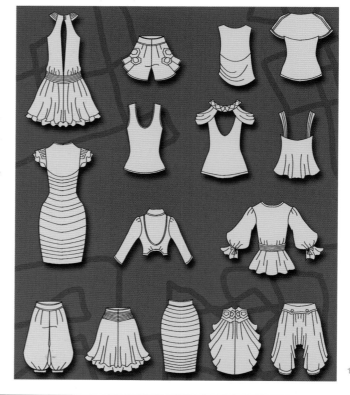

1

2

4

3

Concept board

Concept boards can take the place of a mood board when a context is set for a project or collection. A concept board might also include references to colour palettes with accompanying inspiration or direction images. Concept boards may be used for industry-linked projects, known as 'live' projects, to introduce the design boards that will follow. They sometimes combine the purposes of both a mood board and a colour board, with the additional focus of a context, and should be visually engaging and well-composed.

Title board

This board can sometimes take the place of a mood board if a context is already set and the student wants the focus of their work to be linked to a collection title or theme. Typically, more advanced fashion design students will use a title board to introduce their work in conjunction with other boards such as colour boards, development boards and subsequent artwork or design boards. Title boards can be used to good effect for introducing a project within a portfolio.

1–4 Flats board (1), mood or concept board (2) and illustration boards (3–4) by Lucy Chiu.

Flats board

Although some designers include flats with their illustrations, it is often appropriate to prepare a separate presentation board for flats and thematically link them to your other boards. In some sections of the fashion industry this is common practice, such as for active sportswear and product categories of menswear. Presenting flats on a separate board can enable a designer to give more artistic expression to an illustration without competing with a flat as part of the same composition. Increasingly, presentation flats are being drawn and coloured with the aid of digital graphics software. If you pursue this approach you should consider how it will work alongside your other boards.

Range plan board

Prepared by design teams in the fashion industry to 'break down' a collection into its constituent parts across product categories or consignment deliveries, range plan boards (or line sheets as they are known in the US), are used to clarify final collections for presentation to sales teams and buyers. These boards utilise presentation flats to clearly show each product style against exact fabric swatches. They might include a style number, season, price and delivery date. Range plan boards may be less familiar to students, who will usually produce smaller line-up sheets drawn on the figure.

1

2

1–4   Illustration boards (1 and 3), flats board (2) and colour board (4) by Lucy Chiu.

Line-up sheet

Used by more advanced fashion students, the purpose of line-up sheets is to present and edit final collections in a line-up format that allows the outfits to be evaluated for their overall look, including their catwalk/runway appeal. The designs are drawn on the figure and not as flats, with attention to styling, fit and proportion. It is important, therefore, that they are drawn to a consistent scale and that the poses are not overly dramatic as the purpose of the line-up sheet is to enable critical evaluation of the capsule collection. They may be included in a final portfolio but should not detract from or duplicate final illustration work.

Colour board

Although colour stories can be conveyed as part of a mood board, theme board or range plan, a separate colour board is sometimes useful. Colour boards are used in industry to clarify exact colours and combinations within a product category or merchandise theme. Colour inspiration is important for students of fashion and fashion knitwear, who often include them within their portfolios and provide additional fabric or yarn samples. It is important, however, to consider colour consistency when producing a colour board as your artwork should be colour matched and the colours accurately represented in your design boards.

3

4

Fashion With A Conscience
Womenswear
Spring/Summer 2009

ADDRESSING SUSTAINABILITY

"Traditional Tradewear"

Royal Society Of Arts

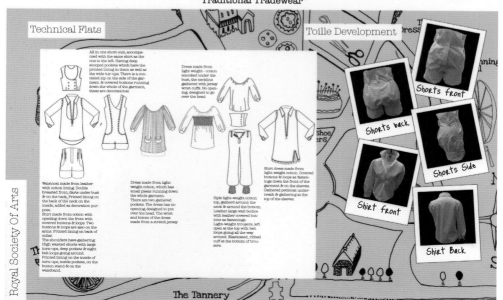

Fashion With A Conscience
Womenswear
Spring/Summer 2009

DEVELOPMENT & TECHNICAL ASPECTS

"Traditional Tradewear"

Royal Society Of Arts

Development board

Some tutors and college professors ask their students to prepare a development board, which visually presents key stages of their development in the studio. This enables students to extract some of their best sketchbook work and combine it with photographic images of toiles/muslins as evidence of their work in progress. Development boards are useful; they can link a mood board to the artwork or final design boards. Although there is no rule on how formally they should be presented, some students include them in their final portfolios.

Illustration board or design board

Fashion illustration boards are an important part of any fashion student or designer's portfolio and are usually among the last to be viewed in the sequence of a portfolio presentation. In one sense they may even be considered to be the finale of a designer's presentation since they serve a more artistic role than the other boards and can add a wow factor to a portfolio. Some designers may include flats with their figurative drawings, while others may adopt a more illustrative format. Determining the format for a fashion illustration is important and should be planned. This includes whether the illustration will be arranged in landscape or portrait format as well as whether to draw more than one figure on the board. Arranging multiple figures can be visually enhancing but should be considered in relation to individual model poses, gender and target market or occasion. For example, illustration boards for bridal wear and high evening wear should emphasise the uniqueness of the design and the occasion, so individual illustrations are more appropriate. Fashion figures can be cropped and framed on illustration boards depending on the desired effect. Composing your illustration is important and, given the variety of approaches to fashion illustration today, you should play to your strengths and emphasise what you can do best.

1–3   Concept board (1),
flats/development board (2)
and illustration/design board
(3) by Miranda Folett-Millard.

3

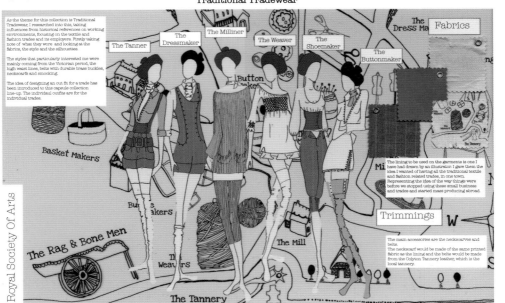

Fashion With A Conscience
Womenswear
Spring/Summer 2009

FINAL COLLECTION

"Traditional Tradewear"

Digital presentations

It is interesting to note the increasing popularity of websites and blogs in which fashion drawings and illustrations are shared and displayed alongside fashion photography and other associated fashion imagery. These digital formats have extended the reach of fashion drawing and presentation styles to a global audience, as well as assimilating them into a digital cultural mix that appears open and receptive to the variety of fashion drawing styles that exist today.

Blogs are also being taken up by fashion students who are actively using them to network and promote their work through online forums and digital gallery spaces. These developments are consistent with the advances in digital graphics software, meaning that fashion drawings are increasingly being viewed through screen-based platforms as well as through a range of print media formats. The continuing influence of digital media for fashion drawings and presentations is likely to remain strong in the foreseeable future. Graphics software, scanners and digital cameras are becoming more sophisticated and a growing number of successful illustrators and designers are using digital media either exclusively or in combination with hand-rendering techniques. If fashion is about creating an ideal and capturing the current mood and spirit of its age, then the digital presentation of fashion artworks will continue to exert a powerful influence over popular culture.

1   Fashion designer and illustrator Richard Haines's blog <www.designermanwhatisawtoday.blogspot.com>

2   The work of fashion illustrator Danny Roberts is frequently featured on blogs and websites.

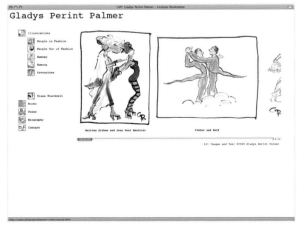

3   Fashion illustrator Gladys Perint Palmer showcases her work on her website <www.gladysperintpalmer.com>

Cecilia Carlstedt, fashion illustrator

Please describe your current job
I work as a freelance illustrator.

**What artistic training
have you had?**
I have always drawn since I was
a young girl, but I began my formal
studies in art at a school called
Södra Latins Gymnasium in
Stockholm. I continued with more
theoretical education, studying art
history for a year at Stockholm
University. In 1998 I was accepted
on to the Graphic Design Foundation
course at the London College of
Printing. This led to a BA in the same
subject specialising in experimental
image-making. The course also
offered a five-month exchange
programme at The Fashion Institute
of Technology in New York.

**How would you describe your
fashion illustration style?**
Experimental, eclectic and with
a love for contrasts.

**What type of media do
you like to use?**
I mix traditional media like pencil
and ink in combination with modern
techniques including Illustrator,
Photoshop and photography.

**How important are computer
graphics in your work?**
It has become increasingly
important over time. I still prefer
a handmade look, but I have to
admit to being quite reliant on the
computer in the process.

**What advice do you have for a
student who wants to work as
a fashion illustrator?**
Experiment a lot with different media
to create your personal style. Always
keep updated on what's going on in
the field.

**What makes a great
fashion illustration?**
For me it's when you can see
that the creator has captured the
essence of the piece in a unique,
confident way.

What or who inspires you?
When I see something that
triggers the nerve to create; that
could be anything really, an unusual
colour combination, an interesting
face, and so on.

Artists who inspire me are many,
but to name a few: Elizabeth Peyton,
Luc Tuymans, Aubrey Beardsley,
Hokusai and Gustav Klimt.

1–2   Illustrations by
Cecilia Carlstedt.

Digital presentations > **Cecilia Carlstedt > Luis Tinoco**

Cecilia Carlstedt, fashion illustrator

1

1–2   Illustrations by
         Cecilia Carlstedt.

Digital presentations > Cecilia Carlstedt > Luis Tinoco

Luis Tinoco, fashion illustrator

**Please describe your
current job as an illustrator**
I am currently working on different
media projects based in different
countries. I usually work with
fashion magazines, newspapers
and textbooks. Basically I try to get
as close as I can to each target
audience; not only do I adapt my
style to each one of them, but I
also preserve the same essence
according to my own style and
technique.

**What artistic training
have you had?**
Illustration has always been a
hobby for me. I remember loving to
draw when I was younger and ever
since I have been furthering my
interest in it. This was by learning
several techniques such as painting,
watercolouring, charcoal drawing
and so on. However, I believe that
my degree in graphic design perhaps
has helped me the most in the
creation of images, not only to
compose and colour them but also
to interpret and reflect them in
images, ideas or concepts.

**How would you describe your
fashion illustration style?**
I would not define it as just one
pure style. To my understanding,
fashion is in constant progress,
always changeable, and my work
acclimatises to it. The same
would apply to the designers –
transformation and evolution is
unstoppable. I would say that the
real challenge is to reproduce that
evolution on a piece of paper.

1–2 Illustrations by Luis Tinoco
    for *Glamour* Germany.

Cecilia Carlstedt > **Luis Tinoco** > Sandra Suy

Luis Tinoco, fashion illustrator

What type of media do you like to use?

I like using any possible method when illustrating. To achieve that, I explore new ways of expression. The mixture (or collage) of different plastic techniques is my main instrument. The results are more rewarding and innovative if I show certain versatility.

How important are computer graphics in your work?

I use the computer together with other methods. I do use it but not primarily. In order to get hold of realistic results and postures with personality and individuality the use of drawing is needed.

What advice do you have for a student who wants to work as a fashion illustrator?

Try to find a unique style that you feel comfortable with and stick to it. It will become your trademark and it is what will make you different from the rest. Also try to build a type of work that would suggest your personality and your life's vision.

What makes a great fashion illustration?

Elegance and strength are two essential elements that need to be considered when working on fashion-related illustrations. Moreover, they are key to making someone stop, pay attention to it and hopefully, keep it in the mind. At the end of the day, it is all about the transmission of feelings beyond what is merely visual.

Who or what inspires you?

I always try to be aware of absolutely everything that takes place around me. Anything could be an inspiration to me: people I see in the street, music, TV, photo sessions...

I also love to pay attention to artists who have lived in a different period. I think that if we still remember them it must be because they have done something good with their lives and the job they did. Perhaps this is why my illustrations have been defined sometimes as being a bit 'retro', which is a real compliment to me.

1–2   Illustrations by Luis Tinoco
for *Glamour* Spain.

Cecilia Carlstedt > **Luis Tinoco** > Sandra Suy

Sandra Suy, fashion illustrator

**Please describe your
current job as an illustrator**
I work with different types of clients,
basically related to fashion, and
usually with very tight deadlines
so I have to work quickly.

**What artistic training
have you had?**
I studied art and fashion design for
five years. The rest of my training
has been on my own.

**How would you describe your
fashion illustration style?**
It's influenced by classic fashion
illustration and I like thinking it's
elegant and reflects beauty in a
good way.

**What type of media do
you like to use?**
In the beginning I used all kind of
artistic media, but now I've achieved
the same effects with my computer,
and it's more comfortable.

1

1–2   Illustrations by Sandra Suy.

2

Sandra Suy, fashion illustrator

How important are computer graphics in your work?
Very important, I use a computer in all my work processes.

What advice do you have for a student who wants to work as a fashion illustrator?
The most important thing is to find your own style and promote your work a lot so people can see it. The internet is a good tool for this.

What makes a great fashion illustration?
Something I can't describe that makes you feel like you're in front of something special.

Who or what inspires you?
My inspiration depends on the moment; it could be an idea or a person who is different from the rest. I try to impregnate my illustrations with the attitude of the moment.

2

1–2   Illustrations by Sandra Suy.

'You are only as good as the people you dress.'

Halston

The final chapter considers the assembly and organisation of fashion drawing and associated artwork boards as part of a visual portfolio. Practical considerations, such as the selection and size of a portfolio case, are discussed along with approaches to the selection and organisation of work within a portfolio. The evolving nature of what may be considered as a fashion portfolio in today's rapidly changing digital media age is also considered, with a speculative eye on the future of fashion. The chapter concludes with an informative interview with the owner and director of a UK-based fashion careers company that offers support and advice on fashion portfolios to students, recent graduates and industry professionals.

What is a fashion portfolio?

Nearly all fashion students will be familiar with the term fashion portfolio. There is really no such thing as a 'one size fits all' model in defining a portfolio: they come in a variety of sizes and formats and contain individual presentations and statements of work that reflect achievement, growth and ambition.

Accepting that fashion portfolios do vary, we might also conclude that they serve a variety of functions. A portfolio is an important visual self-promotion and sales tool for any designer, fashion student or creative individual. There are areas of good practice that we shall consider in relation to preparing and editing a portfolio; as an underlying principle the portfolio should be a key indicator of your creative abilities, strengths and subject interests. In this way it should demonstrate what you do best.

A portfolio should evolve and remain relevant to your experiences and interests. For students they represent a record of learning and achievement that will support career planning and preparation. It is probably fair to say that without a portfolio, a fashion design student would find it almost impossible to secure employment within the fashion industry.

WINTER 2509 BC

Show Hyères

AUTUMN/WINTER 2509 BC

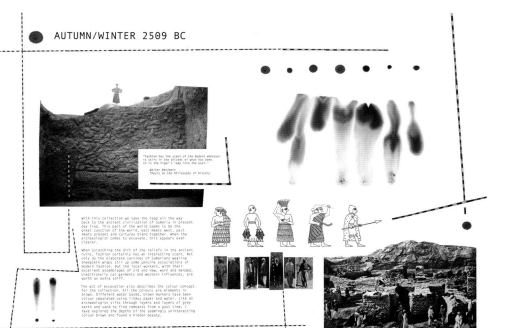

"Fashion has the scent of the modern wherever
it stirs in the thicket of what has been.
It is the tiger's leap into the past."

Walter Benjamin
Thesis on the Philosophy of History

With this collection we take the leap all the way
back to the ancient civilization of Sumeria in present
day Iraq. This part of the world seems to be the
great junction of the world, east meets west, past
meets present and cultures blend together. When the
archaeologist comes to excavate, this appears even
clearer.

When scratching the dirt of the reliefs in the ancient
ruins, fashion certainly has an interesting scent. Not
only do the elaborate carvings of Sumerians wearing
sheepskin wraps stir up some genuine associations of
modern fashion. But the local workers, with their
excellent assemblages of old and new, worn and mended,
traditionally cut garments and western influences, are
worth an extra sniff.

The act of excavation also describes the colour concept
for the collection. All the colours are elements in
brown. Different water based, brown markers have been
colour separated using litmus paper and water. Like an
archaeologist sifts through layers and layers of grey
earth and sand to find remnants from a past time, I
have explored the depths of the seemingly uninteresting
colour brown and found a hidden beauty.

2

WORN AND MENDED

This jacket has a story. Perhaps
has it been handed down from
generation to generation, holes
have been mended untill whole
parts have had to be changed.
The sleeves from another jacket
have been stuck on, the buttons
replaced by a practical zipper,
new patch pockets sewn on top...

Wide collar and lapels,
asymmetrically placed,
zippered patch pockets,
patches on collar and
elbows.

Initial patterns
with extra volume
to be belted in at
top and slim legs.

Lower crotch, almost down
to knee level. A long button
fly sharpens up the trouser
and focuses the shape.

Close to final toile.

The details and shapes from the Levi's denim
have been softened, dropped and adapted to go
with the well worn feel of the clothes worn
in the excavation site.

EAST MEETS WEST

The area where the
Sumerians dwelled seems
to be on the line
which separates the
western and the eastern
hemispheres. Cultures
collide and the
result is a fantastic
bricolage of dress
elements. A western
tailored jackets,
or perhaps a denim
jacket with cutoff
sleeves, worn over a
long kaftan or loose,
draped trousers, check
shirts combined with
white head scarves or
elaborate turbans.

The collar is dropped, the breast
pocket sit lower, the volume is
short, wide and loose, the shoulder
is round and soft.

The Levi's denim jacket and 501 jeans must be some of the
globally most recognizable garments. Like the workers here
incorporate western elements in their wardrobe, the Levi's
garments can be found in wardrobes all over the world with
just as natural a belonging as the Iraqi men make their
tailored jackets seem here.

3

Presentation cases

Selecting a portfolio presentation case is a matter of individual choice for students and designers alike. Fashion students would be well advised to invest in a suitable portfolio case before entering their final year as this will enable them to start organising and collating their project work.

Portfolio cases come in a variety of sizes including A4 and A2 (see page 166 for a conversion table). Fashion design students will use A3 the most. Black cases are generally preferred as they appear business-like and professional. Most portfolio cases are sold in leather-effect PVC with protective gilt corners and strap handles. Additional features may include a shoulder strap, retractable handle, multi-ring mechanism for inserting clear plastic wallets or sleeves and a strong, all round zipper and internal pocket for inserting documents such as a CV/résumé. It is worth remembering that while your portfolio should appear smart and functional it should not upstage the work inside it. A deluxe portfolio case cannot make up for inferior artwork.

1

2

1   Portfolios on display at Graduate Fashion Week, London.

2   Portfolio Open Day at the British Fashion Council colleges forum.

Content and organisation

Content and organisation are key to a successful portfolio. Considering how you present your work is just as important as deciding what to include. Both are inextricably linked and can demonstrate your presentation and organisational skills.

Some interviewers flick through portfolios quickly or even work from the back to the front. It is frustrating but it happens so you should make sure that all your work is presentable and that everything has impact. Students are sometimes advised to start and finish with a strong project. For fashion design students their most recent project, or final collection, is likely to be presented first, and it is worth considering a good project to end with too.

The content of a portfolio should flow from one project to another and demonstrate the scope of your selected work to its best advantage. This includes your ability to edit your work. Addressing content and organisation is also about tailoring your portfolio to a defined audience. Although there are no fixed rules on how many projects should be included within a fashion portfolio (and your tutors or professors can offer specific guidance), approximately five or six accomplished projects in varying styles and formats should engage the interest of an interviewer. Additional projects may need to be held back and targeted for another interview.

Try colour coding projects by mounting artwork on to a particular colour of cardstock to frame it; this can make a presentation appear more cohesive and define the projects within your portfolio. Consider the visual impact of portfolio sleeve pages that face each other; for example, choosing two illustrations that complement each other, or a line-up of figures arranged across the open spread of the sleeves, will create a wow factor.

Ultimately, your portfolio should represent you in the best possible way but should also be an honest representation of who you are, in relation to your interests, previous experiences and your future goals and aspirations.

Portfolio dos and don'ts

Do

Make sure that your artwork will actually fit into the sleeve pages of your portfolio. It may sound obvious, but some students can overlook this and find themselves trimming or remounting work.

Check that the sleeves within the portfolio are spotlessly clean before you insert your artwork. Good artwork will lose its appeal if the sleeve is marked or dirty.

Be consistent with presentation formats within a project; try not to mix landscape format with portrait format.

Make sure that any digital print artwork is properly pixelated.

Don't

It is a common mistake to think that the more you add to your portfolio the better your chances of someone responding to your work. Your interviewer may actually remember the weaker work over the stronger pieces and it could also be interpreted as an indecisive approach.

Artwork with raised surfaces, such as some types of mixed media artwork with sharp peaks or points, may not be suitable for insertion into a portfolio sleeve.

Fold-out presentations may look appealing when they're standing upright on a table surface but do not work within the sleeve of a portfolio so are best avoided.

Try to avoid including isolated mood boards.

Finally, if you're not happy with your work you shouldn't include it in your final portfolio as it is never good practice to apologise for work during an interview.

Digital portfolios

1   *Chew Magazine* is an online magazine; this issue features the illustrations of Sandra Suy. <www.dripbook.com/chewthemagazine>

2   Example of designer's digital portfolio on host site Coroflot. <www.coroflot.com>

As we have seen, documenting and presenting fashion artwork and associated imagery across a variety of digital formats is becoming increasingly widespread and better understood in the context of developing a portfolio.

Both the development of digital photography and the growth of fashion websites have raised the profile of fashion imagery across a variety of digital platforms. The emergence of online fashion magazines, such as *Chew Magazine*, has also extended the reach and accessibility of fashion images. This includes the presentation of drawings and artwork through screen-based rather than print-based platforms. Today, fashion illustrators, designers and students are populating the internet and presenting examples of their work through digital media such as websites, blogs and Flickr image pages. This is leading to some interesting developments, which are beginning to extend the idea of what a fashion portfolio is and what it might look like in the future.

The term e-portfolio is gaining acceptance in a business networking context. Design-orientated websites such as <www.coroflot.com> specifically cater for creative professionals and students across areas of design, including fashion, by enabling them to present digital portfolios of their work with microblogging and profile-linking capabilities, as well as enabling direct access to their portfolio settings and visitor traffic statistics.

The efficient nature of e-portfolios, combined with their rapid digital communication capabilities, makes them highly versatile and compatible with a 24/7 global fashion culture in a way that may not be achieved through a physical portfolio alone. It remains, however, that some of the more tactile human elements of original hand-drawn artwork cannot be conveyed by the digitisation process.

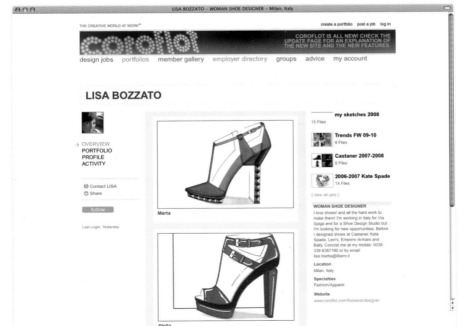

1

2

Stephanie Finnan, fashion careers adviser

Please outline your current job and your career path

My current role is owner and director of The Fashion Careers Clinic, which is the first specialist careers advice service in the UK dedicated to helping fashion, textiles and accessories designers. Based in London, the Clinic provides guidance, direction and support to everyone from new graduates through to experienced designers who are looking for their next (or first) role in the industry. We cover a wide range of topics, including portfolio presentation, CV writing, interview technique, and how to network effectively. As we all know, this is such a competitive industry, therefore designers must equip themselves with all of the necessary tools and information required in order for them to stand a better chance of gaining a solid role in design.

What is a fashion portfolio?

A fashion portfolio is a body of work that brings together a selection of the designer's ideas to demonstrate a certain style or vision. A portfolio can include research, sketches, illustrations, photographs and fabric samples and, presented as a whole, should deliver a very clear message as to what the designer is all about.

What advice would you offer to a student to help them prepare a fashion portfolio?

The most important thing to consider is 'does this work have a clear message?' Think about exactly what sector of the market you are appealing to, and consider if your work is genuinely suitable for this market. The style of your projects can be changed drastically by how you do your figure illustrations – by changing the hairstyle, make-up, shoes and accessories. All of these

things combine to influence how others view your ability to work at a certain market level. Think about what message your work gives out, and also consider how memorable your work is. What makes it stand out? What's different about it? The best portfolios are the ones people can remember even years later – I recall a great womenswear designer who had a very distinctive way of presenting her work and she was fantastic at figure illustration. Six years later, her work still stands out. Each portfolio should have that clear message, be memorable, cohesive, and projects should flow well from one to another. Focus on quality, not quantity, and make sure that every project is one that you're proud of.

On a practical note, students should remember to include all of the required elements clients and recruiters like to see: mood boards,

1 Stephanie's company The Fashion Careers Clinic. <www.fashioncareers clinic.com>

2 Stephanie offers career and portfolio advice to students.

2

then design development, then final designs (pages should ideally include figure illustrations with flats placed alongside). Try to keep each project balanced with a similar number of pages in each – it doesn't look great to have one project with 15 pages and others with just four pages. Finally, keep your portfolio up to date, and remember that a portfolio is never finished – it should evolve as the months and years go by; it is an ongoing body of work.

How should a fashion student go about choosing a portfolio?
Most professional designers work to A4, which is easiest to present at interview; for some reason, work can look better when it is slightly smaller. Going larger than A3 is impractical in terms of portability. A4 or A3 is also much more user-friendly for the recruiter to flip through, and easier to look at if interviewing in a location

such as a restaurant or cafe (bear in mind that interviews don't always happen at the company HQ, or even somewhere with a nice big table to spread all of your work out on!). Choose a style of portfolio that allows you to add and edit work quickly and easily. Some students present their work in a book format, bound into material or casing, or in a box or container. These ways of presentation aren't necessary (they won't make you stand out for the right reasons) and throw up difficulties when having to photocopy pages to send to agencies. The best and most professional-looking portfolios are the leather ones with plastic sleeves already inserted into the spine. The ring binders, where you have to place the plastic sleeves in yourself, invariably look messy as soon as you open them, with some pages falling out or the pages not turning correctly.

Stephanie Finnan, fashion careers adviser

What are the most common mistakes fashion students make when preparing a portfolio?

There are quite a few common mistakes! No clear message is awful. Others include too much or too little work – both as bad as each other. As a general guide, approximately six full projects is about right. Blank pages are not acceptable, nor tatty or messy pages. Check for glue marks, torn pages, smears on plastic sleeves, and make sure that the spelling is correct on all titles, logos and text – clients and recruitment agents do notice all of these things, so double-check everything before you present it.

What is the most important piece of advice you would offer to a fashion student preparing a portfolio for a job interview?

The most important element by far is to make sure that the work presented is actually suitable for the company that is interviewing. Too many designers take a 'one size fits all' approach and take along the same work to lots of different companies. The most successful candidates are those who really think about the style of the company they are interviewing with, research their target market well, and prepare their portfolios accordingly. The best approach would be to create a small project for each company, to present at first interview stage. It doesn't have to be a lot – perhaps a mood board, page of design development and a page of final illustrations. This will show that the candidate has put time and effort into preparing for the interview, rather than assuming that their work will be suitable as it is and going to every interview with the same standard projects.

What role do electronic portfolios serve in fashion?

Electronic portfolios are interesting in that they allow designers to present their work to a much wider audience than ever before. Many designers are choosing to have their own website to promote their work, as well as uploading work to portfolio sites such as Coroflot or StylePortfolios. This allows for a much more immediate and accessible way of presenting work to companies and recruiters globally; it is quite staggering to think that as soon as designers have posted their work on these sites, they could be noticed and contacted by prospective employers on the other side of the world. Electronic portfolios have really changed the face of job hunting for the current generation of designers. However, I do feel that a certain type of work lends itself to this way of presentation more than others; for instance, fashion graphics and print, kidswear and sportswear tends to look better electronically than knitwear, embellishment and work for the luxury market. Some designers are choosing to take a laptop to interviews to present their work, but some companies still prefer to see hard copies of work in a traditional portfolio. Also, presenting with a laptop can bring another set of concerns to the interview situation, such as if the computer crashes, battery dies, files won't open and so on – not an ideal start to an interview!

What do you think fashion portfolios will look like in ten years' time?

As we have seen over the past couple of years, the use of CAD work has become much more prevalent and is now widely requested by the majority of clients. Work created on the computer can look amazing if done correctly; at the moment it is best mixed with other ways of rendering fabric and presenting illustrations, combined with hand-drawn work. I think CAD packages are becoming ever more sophisticated in terms of the effects that can be created, ease of use, and how realistic the final images look; this will continue at a fast pace. In ten years' time the majority of, if not all, portfolios will be created using CAD. Sadly, this may further contribute to the loss of traditional methods of hand drawing and illustration. Following on from the last question, I think that the traditional way of presenting work in a solid portfolio will die out and most designers will present electronic portfolios. Technology will have moved on so much that I'm sure there will be easier and slicker ways for candidates to present their work.

1–3 Stephanie offers career and portfolio advice to students.

2–3

Digital portfolios > Stephanie Finnan

Conclusion

1   Illustration by Lovisa Burfitt.

Fashion drawing encompasses a vibrant and diverse visual vocabulary. We have taken an introductory journey from its beginnings in the 19th century to the variety of styles and applications that constitute fashion drawing in the early 21st century. It is clear that both fashion and drawing continue to be shaped by an evolving aesthetic, by technological advances in computer graphics and by the practical requirements of the fashion industry.

Fashion drawing enables us to define and redefine the way that we see others and ourselves. While drawing remains a practical means for generating or communicating an idea, it should also allow us to dream and to imagine what we want to share with others. Fashion drawing may therefore be considered as a journey of self-discovery that is fed by our imagination and ideas and refined with regular practice. It is important to practise drawing in order to be able to confidently express ideas and test the boundaries.

Of course, it has only been possible to include a select number of drawings by contemporary designers and illustrators in this book, alongside examples by talented students who are setting out on their careers, but their work offers us a slice of contemporary fashion practice. A number of insightful interviews has helped us to understand the motivations and inspirations behind a range of different approaches to fashion drawing and illustration. I hope this book has stimulated your interest in fashion drawing and that it will inspire you to draw.

THE LEARNING CENTRE
CITY & ISLINGTON COLLEGE
444 CAMDEN ROAD
LONDON N7 0SP
TEL: 020 7700 8642

1

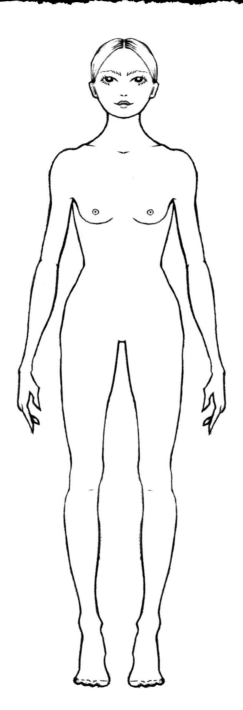

Front template of eight-heads female

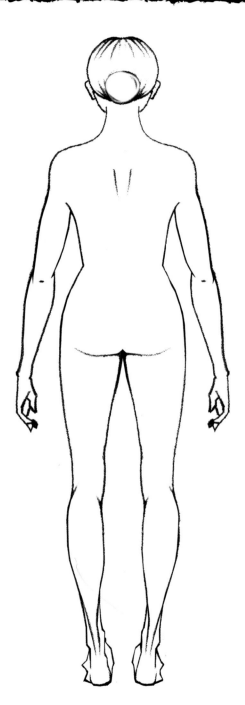

Back template of eight-heads female

Templates

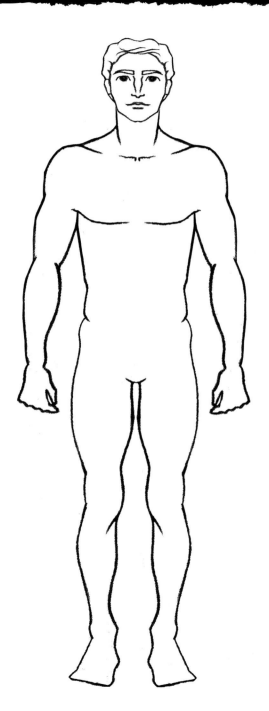

Front template of eight-heads male

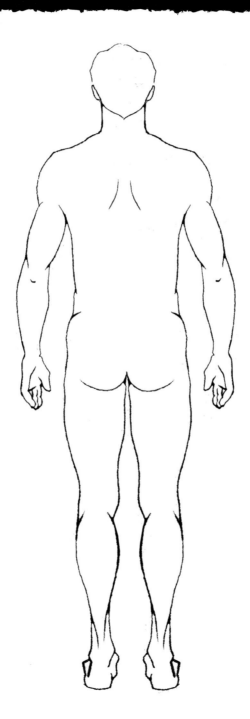

Back template of eight-heads male

In this book we refer to A4 and A3 paper sizes, which are part of the ISO (International Organization for Standardization) A-series. This metric-based system is used throughout the world, except in the US and Canada. For the benefit of North American readers, the table below shows both imperial and metric measurements of the A-series.

Sheet name	mm	inches
A0	841 x 1189	33 x 46¾
A1	594 x 841	23⅜ x 33
A2	420 x 594	16½ x 23⅜
A3	297 x 420	11¾ x 16½
A4	210 x 297	8¼ x 11¾
A5	148 x 210	5⅞ x 8¼
A6	105 x 148	4⅛ x 5⅞
A7	74 x 105	2⅞ x 4⅛
A8	52 x 75	2 x 2⅞

US Letter is the closest equivalent to A4:

	mm	inches
A4	210 x 297	8¼ x 11¾
Letter	216 x 279	8½ x 11

US Tabloid/Ledger is the closest equivalent to A3:

	mm	inches
A3	297 x 420	11¾ x 16½
Tabloid	279 x 432	11 x 17

Fashion Drawing

Illustration by Lovisa Burfitt.

1

Acknowledgements and picture credits

I would like to thank all the contributors who have so generously and willingly agreed to include examples of their work in this book. Thank you for your cooperation and open-handedness. Through the process of writing this book I have been fortunate to meet some inspiring and creative practitioners as well as having the opportunity to renew existing contacts and acquaintances.

In alphabetical order, I would especially like to thank all my interviewees for their professionalism and generous spirit: Petra Börner, Lovisa Burfitt, Cecilia Carlstedt, Stephanie Finnan, Elmaz Hüseyin, Tomek Sowacki, Sandra Suy, Howard Tangye and Luis Tinoco.

I would also like to thank Lectra®, SnapFashun© and Trendstop® for their additional cooperation and support by providing me with a selection of images for this book.

Special thanks also to Holly-Mae Gooch and Helena Kruczynska who both produced original artwork and drawings for this book. It was great working with both of you. My sincere thanks to Richard Haines for generously supplying me with images of his work desk and for his inspiring blog! And thanks to Wendy Plovmand for her generous cooperation and inspirational collages!

Additional thanks to Heather Holford, Sachiko Honda, Cecilia Langemar and David Potts for their help with facilitating contacts for inclusion in this book, and to Carl and Daniel at Sifer Design.

Finally a special thank you to my editor Rachel Netherwood for her tireless help and support. It's been an inspiring journey.

Picture credits

BASICS
FASHION DESIGN

Working with ethics

Lynne Elvins
Naomi Goulder

Publisher's note

The subject of ethics is not new, yet its consideration within the applied visual arts is perhaps not as prevalent as it might be. Our aim here is to help a new generation of students, educators and practitioners find a methodology for structuring their thoughts and reflections in this vital area.

AVA Publishing hopes that these **Working with ethics** pages provide a platform for consideration and a flexible method for incorporating ethical concerns in the work of educators, students and professionals. Our approach consists of four parts:

The **introduction** is intended to be an accessible snapshot of the ethical landscape, both in terms of historical development and current dominant themes.

The **framework** positions ethical consideration into four areas and poses questions about the practical implications that might occur. Marking your response to each of these questions on the scale shown will allow your reactions to be further explored by comparison.

The **case study** sets out a real project and then poses some ethical questions for further consideration. This is a focus point for a debate rather than a critical analysis so there are no predetermined right or wrong answers.

A selection of **further reading** for you to consider areas of particular interest in more detail.

Ethical: awareness/ reflection/ debate

Working with ethics

Introduction

Ethics is a complex subject that interlaces the idea of responsibilities to society with a wide range of considerations relevant to the character and happiness of the individual. It concerns virtues of compassion, loyalty and strength, but also of confidence, imagination, humour and optimism. As introduced in ancient Greek philosophy, the fundamental ethical question is *what should I do?* How we might pursue a 'good' life not only raises moral concerns about the effects of our actions on others, but also personal concerns about our own integrity.

In modern times the most important and controversial questions in ethics have been the moral ones. With growing populations and improvements in mobility and communications, it is not surprising that considerations about how to structure our lives together on the planet should come to the forefront. For visual artists and communicators it should be no surprise that these considerations will enter into the creative process.

Some ethical considerations are already enshrined in government laws and regulations or in professional codes of conduct. For example, plagiarism and breaches of confidentiality can be punishable offences. Legislation in various nations makes it unlawful to exclude people with disabilities from accessing information or spaces. The trade of ivory as a material has been banned in many countries. In these cases, a clear line has been drawn under what is unacceptable.

But most ethical matters remain open to debate, among experts and lay-people alike, and in the end we have to make our own choices on the basis of our own guiding principles or values. Is it more ethical to work for a charity than for a commercial company? Is it unethical to create something that others find ugly or offensive?

Specific questions such as these may lead to other questions that are more abstract. For example, is it only effects on humans (and what they care about) that are important, or might effects on the natural world require attention too?

Is promoting ethical consequences justified even when it requires ethical sacrifices along the way? Must there be a single unifying theory of ethics (such as the Utilitarian thesis that the right course of action is always the one that leads to the greatest happiness of the greatest number), or might there always be many different ethical values that pull a person in various directions?

As we enter into ethical debate and engage with these dilemmas on a personal and professional level, we may change our views or change our view of others. The real test though is whether, as we reflect on these matters, we change the way we act as well as the way we think. Socrates, the 'father' of philosophy, proposed that people will naturally do 'good' if they know what is right. But this point might only lead us to yet another question: *how do we know what is right?*

You
What are your ethical beliefs?

Central to everything you do will be your attitude to people and issues around you. For some people their ethics are an active part of the decisions they make everyday as a consumer, a voter or a working professional. Others may think about ethics very little and yet this does not automatically make them unethical. Personal beliefs, lifestyle, politics, nationality, religion, gender, class or education can all influence your ethical viewpoint.

Using the scale, where would you place yourself? What do you take into account to make your decision? Compare results with your friends or colleagues.

Your client
What are your terms?

Working relationships are central to whether ethics can be embedded into a project and your conduct on a day-to-day basis is a demonstration of your professional ethics. The decision with the biggest impact is whom you choose to work with in the first place. Cigarette companies or arms traders are often-cited examples when talking about where a line might be drawn, but rarely are real situations so extreme. At what point might you turn down a project on ethical grounds and how much does the reality of having to earn a living affect your ability to choose?

Using the scale, where would you place a project? How does this compare to your personal ethical level?

01 02 03 04 05 06 07 08 09 10

01 02 03 04 05 06 07 08 09 10

Your specifications
What are the impacts of your materials?

In relatively recent times we are learning that many natural materials are in short supply. At the same time we are increasingly aware that some man-made materials can have harmful, long-term effects on people or the planet. How much do you know about the materials that you use? Do you know where they come from, how far they travel and under what conditions they are obtained? When your creation is no longer needed, will it be easy and safe to recycle? Will it disappear without a trace? Are these considerations the responsibility of you or are they out of your hands?

Using the scale, mark how ethical your material choices are.

Your creation
What is the purpose of your work?

Between you, your colleagues and an agreed brief, what will your creation achieve? What purpose will it have in society and will it make a positive contribution? Should your work result in more than commercial success or industry awards? Might your creation help save lives, educate, protect or inspire? Form and function are two established aspects of judging a creation, but there is little consensus on the obligations of visual artists and communicators toward society, or the role they might have in solving social or environmental problems. If you want recognition for being the creator, how responsible are you for what you create and where might that responsibility end?

Using the scale, mark how ethical the purpose of your work is.

01 02 03 04 05 06 07 08 09 10   01 02 03 04 05 06 07 08 09 10

Working with ethics

One aspect of fashion design that raises an ethical dilemma is the way that clothes production has changed in terms of the speed of delivery of products and the now international chain of suppliers. 'Fast fashion' gives shoppers the latest styles sometimes just weeks after they first appeared on the catwalk, at prices that mean they can wear an outfit once or twice and then replace it. Due to lower labour costs in poorer countries, the vast majority of Western clothes are made in Asia, Africa, South America or Eastern Europe in potentially hostile and sometimes inhumane working conditions. It can be common for one piece of clothing to be made up of components from five or more countries, often thousands of miles apart, before they end up in the high-street store. How much responsibility should a fashion designer have in this situation if manufacture is controlled by retailers and demand is driven by consumers? Even if designers wish to minimise the social impact of fashion, what might they most usefully do?

Traditional Hawaiian feather capes (called 'Ahu'ula) were made from thousands of tiny bird feathers and were an essential part of aristocratic regalia. Initially they were red ('Ahu'ula literally means 'red garment') but yellow feathers, being especially rare, became more highly prized and were introduced to the patterning.

The significance of the patterns, as well as their exact age or place of manufacture is largely unknown, despite great interest in their provenance in more recent times. Hawaii was visited in 1778 by English explorer Captain James Cook and feather capes were amongst the objects taken back to Britain.

The basic patterns are thought to reflect gods or ancestral spirits, family connections and an individual's rank or position in society. The base layer for these garments is a fibre net, with the surface made up of bundles of feathers tied to the net in overlapping rows. Red feathers came from the 'i'iwi or the 'apapane. Yellow feathers came from a black bird with yellow tufts under each wing called 'oo'oo, or a mamo with yellow feathers above and below the tail.

Thousands of feathers were used to make a single cape for a high chief (the feather cape of King Kamehameha the Great is said to have been made from the feathers of around 80,000 birds). Only the highest-ranking chiefs had the resources to acquire enough feathers for a full-length cape, whereas most chiefs wore shorter ones which came to the elbow.

The demand for these feathers was so great that they acquired commercial value and provided a full-time job for professional feather-hunters. These fowlers studied the birds and caught them with nets or with bird lime smeared on branches. As both the 'i'iwi and 'apapane were covered with red feathers, the birds were killed and skinned. Other birds were captured at the beginning of the moulting season, when the yellow display feathers were loose and easily removed without damaging the birds.

The royal family of Hawaii eventually abandoned the feather cape as the regalia of rank in favour of military and naval uniforms decorated with braid and gold. The 'oo'oo and the mamo became extinct through the destruction of their forest feeding grounds and imported bird diseases. Silver and gold replaced red and yellow feathers as traded currency and the manufacture of feather capes became a largely forgotten art.

Is it more ethical to create clothing for the masses rather than for a few high-ranking individuals?

Is it unethical to kill animals to make garments?

Would you design and make a feather cape?

Fashion is a form of ugliness so intolerable that we have to alter it every six months.

Oscar Wilde

Working with ethics

AIGA
Design Business and Ethics
2007, AIGA

Eaton, Marcia Muelder
Aesthetics and the Good Life
1989, Associated University Press

Ellison, David
Ethics and Aesthetics in European Modernist Literature:
From the Sublime to the Uncanny
2001, Cambridge University Press

Fenner, David E W (Ed)
Ethics and the Arts:
An Anthology
1995, Garland Reference Library of Social Science

Gini, Al and Marcoux, Alexei M
Case Studies in Business Ethics
2005, Prentice Hall

McDonough, William and Braungart, Michael
Cradle to Cradle:
Remaking the Way We Make Things
2002, North Point Press

Papanek, Victor
Design for the Real World:
Making to Measure
1972, Thames and Hudson

United Nations Global Compact
The Ten Principles
www.unglobalcompact.org/AboutTheGC/TheTenPrinciples/index.html